next door
savior

MAX LUCADO

NEXT DOOR SAVIOR

WITH TEEN STORY ADAPTATIONS BY MONICA HALL

TRANSIT

www.TransitBooks.com
A Division of Thomas Nelson, Inc.
www.ThomasNelson.com

For Jeremy and Lara Shipp—
offering a standing "O" in honor of
your love for God's kids.

NEXT DOOR SAVIOR STUDENT EDITION (WITH TEEN STORY ADAPTATIONS BY MONICA HALL)

Text copyright © 2004 Max Lucado.

Published in Nashville, Tennessee, by Tommy Nelson®, a Division of Thomas Nelson, Inc.

Karen Hill, Administrative Editor for Max Lucado.

Interior Design by Brecca Theele.

Unless otherwise noted, Scripture quotations used in this book are from the New American Standard Bible (NASB), © 1960, 1977, 1995 by the Lockman Foundation.

Other Scripture references are used by permission from the following sources:

The Amplified Bible (AMP) Old Testament, copyright © 1965, 1987 by The Zondervan Corporation; The Amplified New Testament, copyright © 1954, 1958, 1987 by The Lockman Foundation. The Contemporary English Version (CEV) copyright © 1991 by the American Bible Society. The International Children's Bible®, New Century Version® (ICB), copyright © 1986, 1989, 1999 by Tommy Nelson®, a Division of Thomas Nelson, Inc. The King James Version of the Bible (KJV). The Living Bible (TLB), copyright © 1971 by Tyndale House Publishers. The Message (MSG), copyright © 1993, 1994, 1995 by Eugene H. Peterson, NavPress Publishing Group. New Century Version® (NCV), copyright © 1987, 1988, 1991 by Word Publishing, a Division of Thomas Nelson, Inc. The Holy Bible, New International Version (NIV), copyright © 1973, 1978, 1984, International Bible Society, Zondervan Bible Publishers. The New King James Version® (NKJV®), copyright 1979, 1980, 1982, Thomas Nelson, Inc. The Holy Bible, New Living Translation (NLT), copyright © 1996 by Tyndale House Publishers, Inc. The New Revised Standard Version Bible (NRSV), copyright © 1989 by the Division of Christian Education of the National Council of the Churches of Christ in the USA. The Revised Standard Version of the Bible (RSV), copyright © 1946, 1952, and 1971 by the Division of Christian Education of the National Council of the Churches of Christ in the USA.

Library of Congress Cataloging-in-Publication Data

Lucado, Max
    Next door Savior / by Max Lucado ; with teen story adaptations by Moncia Hall.
      p. cm.
    Based on Next Door Savior by Max Lucado.
    ISBN: 1-4003-0372-9
    BV4501.3 .L85 2004   2003023247

Printed in the United States of America
04 05 06 07 08 PHX 5 4 3 2 1

contents

Acknowledgments ~~~~~~~~~~~~~~~~~~~~~~~~~ viii

A Letter from Max Lucado ~~~~~~~~~~~~~~~~~~~~ ix

1. Our Next Door Savior ~~~~~~~~~~~~~~~~~~~~ 1
   Matthew 16:13–16

part one
NO PERSON HE WON'T TOUCH

2. Christ's Theme Song ~~~~~~~~~~~~~~~~~~~ 17
   (Every Person)
   Hebrews 2:17–18

3. Friend of Outcasts ~~~~~~~~~~~~~~~~~~~~~ 30
   (Shady People)
   Matthew 9:9–13

4. The Trashman ~~~~~~~~~~~~~~~~~~~~~~~~ 43
   (Imperfect People)
   John 1:29

5. Try Again ~~~~~~~~~~~~~~~~~~~~~~~~~~ 54
   (Discouraged People)
   Luke 5:1–11

6. Spit Therapy ~~~~~~~~~~~~~~~~~~~~~~~ 69
    (Suffering People)
    John 9:1–38

7. It's Not Up to You ~~~~~~~~~~~~~~~~~~~ 83
    (Spiritually Confused People)
    John 3:1–16

Part Two
NO PLACE HE WON'T GO

8. He Loves to Be with the Ones He Loves ~~~~~99
    (Everyplace)
    Philippians 2:5–7

9. A Cure for the Common Life ~~~~~~~~~~~ 109
    (Ordinary Places)
    Mark 6:3

10. Oh, to Be DTP-Free! ~~~~~~~~~~~~~~~~~ 121
    (Places of the Heart)
    Luke 2:41–49

11. From Shopper to Buyer ~~~~~~~~~~~~~~~134
    (Unexpected Places)
    Matthew 3:13–17

12. The Long, Lonely Winter ~~~~~~~~~~~~~ 144
    (Wilderness Places)
    Luke 4:1–13

13. God Gets into Things ~~~~~~~~~~~~~~~~ 158
    (Stormy Places)
    Matthew 14:22–33

14. Christ's Point of View ~~~~~~~~~~~~~~~~ 170
    (God-Blessed Places)
    Luke 21:37

15. Still in the Neighborhood ~~~~~~~~~~~~~~184
    (Near Enough to Touch. Strong Enough to Trust.)
    Matthew 28:20

Notes ~~~~~~~~~~~~~~~~~~~~~~~~~~~~~~~~~ 197

ACKNOWLEDGMENTS

Many thanks to these special folks:

* Monica Hall—for finely crafted stories.
* Beverly Phillips—for thoughtfully shepherding the project.
* June Ford—for careful "tweaking."
* Katelin Christopher and Joel Warren—thanks for reading the manuscript and sharing your ideas.
* And especially for Jesus, our next door Savior.

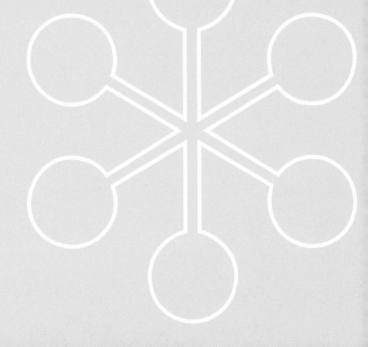

Dear Friend,

Have you ever wondered just who Jesus really is? If you have, you're not alone. Generations have pondered this question, Jesus' own followers puzzled over it. I can remember sitting in a classroom, my mind filled with questions about Jesus.

Then a teacher shared a simple message: If Jesus is who he claimed to be, eternal salvation belongs to those who believe in him. Wow! What an extraordinary fact. From that moment on, I wanted to learn all I could about this God who became a man just so you and I could spend eternity with him.

I pray that this book helps you in your desire to know and understand what I call the "God-man Jesus"—at the same time God and man. Near enough to touch. Strong enough to trust. A next door Savior.

Max Lucado

chapter 1

our next door savior

MATTHEW 16:13-16

Now when Jesus came into the district of Caesarea Philippi, He was asking His disciples, "Who do people say that the Son of Man is?" And they said, "Some say John the Baptist; and others, Elijah; but still others, Jeremiah, or one of the prophets." He said to them, "But who do you say that I am?" Simon Peter answered, "You are the Christ, the Son of the living God."

—Matthew 16:13–16

❋ ❋ ❋ The words hang in the air like a just-rung bell. "Who do you say that I am?" Silence settles on the horseshoe of followers. Nathanael clears his throat. Andrew ducks his eyes. John chews on a fingernail. Judas splits a blade of grass. He won't speak up. Never does. Peter will. Always does.

But he pauses first. Jesus' question is not new to him.

The previous thousand times, however, Peter has kept the question to himself.

That day in Nain? He'd asked it. Most stand quietly as funeral processions pass. Mouths closed. Hands folded. Reverently silent. Not Jesus. He approached the mother of the dead boy and whispered something in her ear that made her turn and look at her son. She started to object but didn't. Signaling to the pallbearers, she instructed, "Wait."

Jesus walked toward the boy. Eye-level with the corpse, he spoke. Not over it, as a prayer, but to it, as a command. "Young man, I say to you, arise!" (Luke 7:14).

With the tone of a teacher telling students to sit or the authority of a mom telling kids to get out of the rain, Jesus commanded the dead boy *not to be dead*. And the boy obeyed. Cold skin warmed. Stiff limbs moved. White cheeks colored. The men lowered the coffin, and the boy jumped up and into his mother's arms. Jesus "gave him back to his mother" (Luke 7:15).

Just who are you?

An hour later Jesus and the guys were eating the evening meal. He laughed at a joke and asked for seconds on bread, and the irony of it all jolted Peter. *"Who are you?"* he wondered so softly that no one but God could hear. *You just awakened the dead! Should you not be encased in light or encircled by angels or enthroned higher than a thousand Caesars? Yet, look at you— wearing clothes I would wear and laughing at jokes I tell and eating the food we all eat. Is this what death defeaters do? Just who are you?*

Just who do you think you are . . . Spiderman?!

Matt Harris was in trouble. And he knew it. Fingers jammed into the narrow crack above his head . . . toes barely clinging to the shallow ledge beneath him . . . he hugged the sheer moonlit face of Desperation Bluff. Couldn't go up. Couldn't go down. More to the point, couldn't hang on *here*—fifty feet above the ground—much longer, either. And since—against every rule—he was climbing alone, at night, with no safety line, he was well and truly stuck.

What was I thinking?! That was the problem, of course: He *hadn't* been thinking. But he'd certainly been talking. Again.

You might call it confidence. You might call it bravado. And you might be right—either way. Whenever Matt was faced with a challenge, his immediate reaction was always, "No problem. I can do that." And, though he had little to say otherwise, he had no hesitation at all about speaking up on those occasions.

Run faster, swim farther, hike longer, climb higher than anyone else at camp? "No problem." And the thing was—thanks to his superb coordination, stubborn determination, *and* a lot of hard work—he'd pull it off! Of course, there *were* the occasional "white-knuckle" moments here and there—or, to be honest, here and *now*.

Think, Matt! You got yourself into this. Now it's up to you to deal with it—like always. After all, who *else* could he count on? Experience had taught him the answer to that question: nobody!

Blinking the sweat from his eyes, Matt searched the rockface one more time. Was that a foothold off to his right? And, could he reach it? Just as he stretched his foot out carefully to test the possibility . . . the moon was swallowed by a cloud. In fact, there were suddenly a *lot* of clouds—big, billowy, *thunderstorm* clouds—barreling his way!

Okay, slight complication. But I didn't expect it to be easy. On the other hand, Matt's impromptu midnight practice had been exactly that at first: easy. Slipping from his bunk after "lights out"; finding his way to the climbing area by the light of a brilliant full moon; his first cautious moves across the bottom of Desperation Bluff—easy. So easy, in fact, that Matt was lured into attempting more than he had intended.

He'd only planned to get the "feel" of the climb with a little bouldering—moving sideways across the rockface just a few feet off the ground. That way if he *did* slip and fall, no harm done. But Desperation Bluff offered foothold after foothold, handhold after handhold—each just *slightly* higher than the last. Soon, instead of flowing smoothly *across* the rock, Matt was moving *up*. To his present predicament.

And now—rumbling and grumbling its way closer by the minute—there was the storm.

❉ ❉ ❉ The mystery of who—or what—Jesus was had teased at Peter many times. For instance, there was the storm. The tie-yourself-to-the-mast-and-kiss-your-boat-good-bye storm. Ten-foot waves yanked the disciples first forward and then backward, leaving the boat ankle-deep in water. Matthew's face lost all its color. Thomas death-gripped the stern. Peter suggested that they pray the Lord's Prayer. Better still if the

Lord led them in the Lord's Prayer. That's when he heard the Lord.

Snoring.

Jesus was asleep. Back against the bow. Head dropped forward. Chin flopping on chest as the boat bounced on waves. "Jesus!" Peter shouted.

The carpenter woke up, looked up. He wiped the rain from his eyes, puffed both cheeks with a sigh, and stood. He raised first his hand, then his voice, and as fast as you could say "glassy," the water became just that. Jesus smiled and sat, and Peter stared and wondered. "Who is this? Even the wind and the waves obey him!" (Mark 4:41 NCV).

This time Jesus is the one posing the question: "Who do you say that I am?" (Matthew 16:15).

Perhaps Peter's reply had the tone of an anchorman on the six o'clock news. Arched eyebrow. Half smile. James Bond-ish baritone voice. "I believe that you are the Son of God." But I doubt it.

I'm seeing Peter kick the dirt a bit. Clear his throat. Less swagger, more swallow. Gulp. More like a first-time parachutist about to jump out of the plane. "Are you ready to jump?" he's asked. "I, uh, I, uh, I, uh . . ."

"Who do you say that I am?"

"I, uh, I, uh . . . I believe . . . that you are the Christ, the Son of the living God" (see Matthew 16:16).

If Peter was hesitant, you can hardly fault him. How many times do you call a callous-handed nail bender from a one-camel town the Son of God?

There was something wrong with the picture. Something that didn't quite fit.

Matt was positive he'd never fit into the picture at Adventure Camp when his new parents first brought up the idea. *Me? In the middle of nowhere? Relying on other people? No way!*

Matt could tell that Bill and Nancy Harris knew exactly what he was thinking. And he was sorry for that. He really liked the Harrises and wanted to make this adoption work as much as they did. But after years in the foster-care system—moved from place to place—he'd learned not to count on anything, or anyone, but himself.

> **Matt had learned not to count on anything, or anyone, but himself.**

Matt had a real problem with the whole *trust* thing. And keeping even people he cared about at a distance had become a habit he couldn't seem to break—no matter how hard he tried. That's when the Harrises had come up with the camp idea. They were convinced that a month of sharing fun, adventure—*and* teamwork—with other kids would do a world of good for Matt.

"Look at it this way, kiddo," said Bill Harris with a grin, "what have you got to lose? You like mastering new skills. And you never know when a talent for archery or canoeing or . . . other things . . . might come in handy. Besides, it's a really cool place."

Adventure Camp was everything—and nothing—that Matt had expected.

For one thing, it *was* a really cool place. Rustic bunkhouses tucked beneath tall pines on the shores of a crystal mountain lake—what was there *not* to like?!

Every day was filled to the brim with the promised adventure: Hiking. Canoeing. Sailing. Survival challenges. Overnight campouts. And Matt's personal favorite . . . free climbing.

And the other kids? Well, they seemed nice enough, and Matt was an old hand at getting along . . . without actually getting involved. Besides, he was so busy that there wasn't a lot of time to wonder about fitting in. Except . . .

If only there weren't so many group *activities.* Matt still had reservations about those. Though he did have to admit that other hands were, well, handy—even essential—on a tug-of-war rope, or trimming racing sails, or belaying a safety line during a rock climb. *And just try running those obstacle course relays all by yourself, Matt my boy!*

So, though he doubted he'd ever be a team player, Matt gave it his best try—and hoped that no one would notice his discomfort.

Of course, they did notice. And wonder. In fact, the other kids still weren't quite sure *what* to make of independent, self-contained Matt. He never started a conversation, but he usually had something interesting to add. Teamwork was definitely *not* his thing, but he always did more than his share. He might never tell a joke, but he certainly got every one he heard. And he was good—very good—at anything he tried.

All of which would be fine—if it weren't for that *annoying*

"No problem" that was Matt's response to each new challenge. And even that was a little puzzling, because his announcements seemed to be aimed more at himself than at them—almost as if he were challenging *Matt*. But that didn't make sense. Did it?

But then again, there were a *lot* of things about Matt that didn't fit the usual picture.

✤ ✤ ✤ There were a lot of things about Jesus that didn't quite fit Peter's view of the world. Kind of like those pictures your teacher used to pass out in grade school. Remember them—the ones with the question at the bottom: "What's wrong with this picture?" You'd look closely for something that didn't fit. A farmyard scene with a piano near the water trough. A classroom with a pirate seated in the back row. An astronaut on the moon with a pay phone in the background. We'd ponder the picture and point to the piano or pirate or pay phone and say, "This doesn't fit." Something is out of place. Something is absurd. Pianos don't belong in farmyards. Pirates don't sit in classrooms. Pay phones aren't found on the moon, and God doesn't chum with the common folk or snooze in fishing boats.

But according to the Bible, he did. "For in Christ there is all of God in a human body" (Colossians 2:9 TLB). Jesus was not a godlike man, nor a manlike God. He was God-man.

- Born in a stable.

- Bathed by a peasant girl.

- The Maker of the world with a belly button.

- The Author of the Torah being taught the Torah.

- Heaven's human. And because he was, we are left with scratch-your-head, double-blink, what's-wrong-with-this-picture? moments like these:

- Wine instead of water.

- A cripple sponsoring the town dance.

- A sack lunch satisfying five thousand tummies.

- And, most of all, a grave: guarded by soldiers, sealed by a rock, yet vacated by a three-days-dead man.

What do we do with such moments?

What do we do with such a *person?* We applaud men for doing good things. We enshrine God for doing great things. But when a man does God things?

One thing is certain, we can't ignore him.

Why would we want to? If these moments are factual, if the claim of Christ is actual, then he was, at once, man and God.

There he was, the single most significant person who ever lived. Forget MVP; he is the entire league. The head of the parade? Hardly. No one else shares the street. Who comes close? Humanity's best and brightest fade like dime-store rubies next to him.

Dismiss him? We can't.

Resist him? Equally difficult. Don't we need a God-man Savior? A just-God Jesus could make us but not understand us. A just-man Jesus could love us but never save us. But a God-man Jesus? Near enough to touch. Strong enough to trust. A next door Savior.

A Savior found by millions to be irresistible. Nothing compares to "the surpassing worth of knowing Christ Jesus my Lord" (Philippians 3:8 RSV). The reward of Christianity is Christ.

Do you journey to the Grand Canyon for the souvenir T-shirt or the snow globe with the snowflakes that fall when you shake it? No. The reward of the Grand Canyon is the Grand Canyon. The wide-eyed realization that you are part of something ancient, splendid, powerful, and greater than you.

The reward of Christianity is Christ. Not money in the bank or a car in the garage or a healthy body or a better self-image. Those things might, or might not, happen. But the Fort Knox of faith is Christ. Fellowshipping with him. Walking with him. Pondering him. Exploring him. The heart-stopping realization that in him you are part of something ancient, endless, unstoppable, and unfathomable. And that he, who can dig the Grand Canyon with his pinkie, thinks you're worth his death on Roman timber. Christ is the reward of Christianity.

If there's a reward for messing up—some kind of "Just Desserts" trophy—I guess it's mine!

Matt's attempt at grim humor was a lot more grim than humorous. Things were not looking good. Nothing he'd tried had worked. And every flash of lightning from the gathering storm only made the picture clearer. He had no place to go. Every crack, crevice, knob, hollow, or infinitesimal ledge remained stubbornly out of reach.

Even worse, the shallow depressions that he clung to were

not all that secure. Oh, they were fine as quick pull-up or push-off points for a body in motion, but as permanent resting places they left a lot to be desired. And when that storm arrived, and they got wet . . .

"Now you know why they call it *Desperation* Bluff," said a calm voice from the darkness.

If he hadn't been practically *glued* to the rock, Matt would have jumped out of his skin. He knew that voice! In fact, it had guided him through the basics of free climbing for the last two weeks.

"Zack?!" Of all the people in the world to find him stuck like this! Zack—everybody's favorite camp counselor and climbing instructor—was someone Matt longed to impress. And instead . . .

"Wh . . . what are you doing here?" Matt blurted.

"I might ask you the same," came the reply.

"Well . . . you know," was all Matt could think of.

Zack did know. When Matt's bunk was empty at bed check, Zack had guessed exactly what was up. What *did* surprise him was just how high "up" was. *Not bad for a beginner. And at least he's wearing his harness—though a rope would have been nice, too!*

"Never mind," said Zack, already climbing smoothly past Matt, "we'll go into that later. For now, just hang in there while I rig our safety lines."

"No . . . no problem," said Matt, listening to the welcome sound of Zack's hammer tapping anchor bolts into the rock above.

A slither of rope and Zack was dangling beside him—barely within reach. "Okay, Matt, this is going to be a little tricky.

Before we can climb down, I've got to get a line attached to your harness. But first, I have to reach you.

"You just have to reach out . . . and trust."

"I'm as close as I can get. When I say so, you're going to have to let go and reach out for my hand, so I can pull over to you. Can you do that?"

Can I? Let go, and put myself entirely in someone else's hands?!

Zack waited patiently through the silence, then, "It's the only way, Matt. Sometimes—when you've lost your way, or gone as far as you can go by yourself—you just have to reach out . . . and *trust*."

Matt took a deep breath—and felt something shift inside himself. Then, "Okay," he said. "No problem." And, when the moment came, Matt reached out in the darkness—and gave himself up to the wonders of trust.

✽ ✽ ✽ Do *you* need a hand to hold in the dark? Someone to count on when things get tough? Jesus is there for you. Always has been. And he's closer than you may ever have dreamed. Don't think so? Let me show you. Let's look at some places he went and some people he touched. Join me on a quest for his "God-manness." You may be amazed.

More important, you may be changed. "We all, with unveiled face, beholding the glory of the Lord, are being changed into his likeness from one degree of glory to another;

for this comes from the Lord who is the Spirit" (2 Corinthians 3:18 RSV).

As we behold him, we become like him.

I experienced this principle firsthand when an opera singer visited our church. We didn't know his voice was trained. You couldn't have known by his corduroy coat and loafers. No tuxedo, cummerbund, or silk tie. His appearance raised no eyebrow, but his voice certainly did. I should know. He was in the pew behind mine.

His vibrato made dentures rattle and rafters shake. He tried to contain himself. But how can a tuba hide in a roomful of piccolos?

For a moment I was startled. But within a verse, I was inspired. Emboldened by his volume, I lifted mine. Did I sing better? Not even I could hear me. My warbles were lost in his talent. But did I try harder? No doubt. His power brought out the best in me.

Could your world use a little music? If so, invite heaven's baritone to cut loose. He may look as common as the guy next door, but just wait till you see what he can do. Who knows? A few songs with him might change the way you sing.

Forever.

Part One

No Person He Won't Touch

Most of us had a hard time learning to tie our shoes. Squirting toothpaste on a brush was tough enough, but tightening shoes by wrapping strings together? Nothing easy about that. Besides, who needs them? Wear loafers. Go barefoot. Who came up with the idea of shoes anyhow?

And knees don't help. Always in your face. Leaning around them, pushing them away—a person can't concentrate.

And, oh, the advice! Everyone had a different approach. "Make a tree with the loop, and let the squirrel run around it into the hole." "Shape a rabbit ear, then wrap it with a ribbon." Dad said, "Go fast." Your uncle said to take your time. Can't anyone agree? Only on one thing. You need to know how.

Learning to tie your shoes is a rite of passage. Right in there with first grade and first bike is first shoe tying. But, oh, how dreadful is the process.

Just when you think you've made the loops and circled the tree . . . you get the rabbit ears in either hand and give them a triumphant yank, and, voilá!—a knot. Unbeknownst to you, you've just been inducted into reality.

My friend Roy used to sit on a park bench for a few minutes each morning. He liked to watch kids gather and play at the bus stop. One day he noticed a little fellow, maybe five or six years of age, struggling to board the bus. While others were climbing on, he was leaning down, frantically trying to untangle a knotted shoestring. He grew more anxious by the moment, frantic eyes darting back and forth between the shoe and the ride.

All of a sudden it was too late. The door closed.

The boy fell back on his haunches and sighed. That's when he saw Roy. With tear-filled eyes he looked at the man on the bench and asked, "Do you untie knots?"

Jesus loves that request.

Life gets tangled. People mess up. You never outgrow the urge to look up and say, "Help!"

Jesus had a way of appearing at such moments. Peter's empty boat. Nicodemus's empty heart. Matthew has a friend issue. A woman has a shame issue. Look who shows up.

Jesus, our next door Savior.

"Do you untie knots?"

"Yes."

Therefore, He had to be made like His brethren in all things, so that He might become a merciful and faithful high priest in things pertaining to God, to make propitiation for the sins of the people. For since He Himself was tempted in that which He has suffered, He is able to come to the aid of those who are tempted.

—Hebrews 2:17–18

❋ ❋ ❋ Most families keep their family secrets a secret. Most don't talk about the swindling uncle or the wayward great-aunt. Such stories remain unmentioned at the family reunion and unrecorded in the family Bible.

That is, unless you are the God-man. Jesus displays the bad apples of his family tree in the first chapter of the New Testament. You've barely dipped a toe into Matthew's Gospel when you realize Jesus hails from the Tilted-Halo Society. Rahab was a Jericho harlot. Grandpa Jacob was slippery enough to qualify for a house-arrest ankle bracelet. David had a personality as irregular as a Picasso painting—one day writing psalms, another day making advances to his captain's wife. But did Jesus erase his name from the list? Not at all.

If your family tree has bruised fruit, then Jesus wants you to know his does, too.

You'd think he would have. *Entertainment Tonight* could dig a season of gossip out of these stories. Why did Jesus hang his family's dirty laundry on the neighborhood clothesline?

Because your family has some, too. An uncle with a prison record. The dad who never came home. The grandparent who ran away with the coworker. If your family tree has bruised fruit, then Jesus wants you to know his does, too. He's been there.

"Get a grip, Jane. It's only a weekend family reunion. You'll get through it . . . somehow." Jane's exasperated sigh became a reluctant smile as her offbeat sense of humor kicked in. *Talking to yourself now, are you? That's a little "out there," even for* this *family.*

The truth was, Jane's big family—from nearest and dearest to most distant kin—sometimes made her feel vaguely . . .

ashamed. Not ashamed of *them!* How could you do anything but admire such an energetic, enthusiastic, excellence-prone bunch? No, it's Jane herself—awkward Jane, studious Jane, *plain* Jane—who often feels shamefully inadequate in this family of exuberant achievers. In fact, Jane occasionally wonders if she was somehow grafted by mistake onto this particular family tree!

Root and branch, the Carlton clan practiced success with a capital *S*. Athletes. Scientists. Authors. Artists. Inventors. Even beauty queens! Name it, and a Carlton somewhere, sometime, had achieved it.

And what does Jane believe she brings to the table? Nada. Zip. Nothing! Even worse, she's going to be displaying her total lack of distinction to her entire extended family at this weekend's Carlton reunion. And, to top things off, she'll be sharing a room with her "perfect" cousin, Lindsey!

Because they live so far apart, Jane and Lindsey haven't seen each other in a long time. But that doesn't mean Jane doesn't know all about Lindsey—who, though only two years older, is outstanding even among the routinely outstanding Carltons. Their moms were dedicated letter writers—which was bad enough—but now they've discovered e-mail, so the entire family is always up to date concerning the ongoing exploits of Lindsey-the-Amazing, complete with pictures.

Jane, who thinks her sole claim to fame is absolutely *no* claim to fame—except possibly a talent for saying the wrong thing at the wrong time—dreads the ordeal ahead. *What will Lindsey and I have to talk about? Our worlds couldn't be farther apart!*

✳ ✳ ✳ Worlds apart. Jesus has been there. Just look at his hometown. A sleepy, humble, forgotten hamlet.

To find its like in our world, where would we go? We'd leave the United States. We'd bypass Europe and most of Latin America. Israel wasn't a superpower or a commercial force or a vacation resort. The land Joshua settled and Jesus loved barely registered on the Roman Empire radar screen! But it was there. Caesar's soldiers occupied it. The Judean hills knew the rumbles of a foreign army. Though you've got to wonder if Roman soldiers ever made it as far north as Nazareth.

Picture a dusty, quiet village. A place that would cause people to say, "Does anything good come out of _____?" In the case of Christ, the blank was filled with the name Nazareth. An unimpressive town in an unimpressive nation.

Where do we go to find such a place today? Iraq? Afghanistan? Cambodia? Take your pick. Find a remote rural area existing on the fringes of modern life. Climb into a Jeep, and go there looking for a family like Jesus'.

Ignore the nicer homes of the village. Joseph and Mary celebrated the birth of Jesus with a temple offering of two turtle-doves, the gift of the poor (Luke 2:22–24). Go to the poorer part of town. Not poverty-stricken or destitute, just simple.

And look for a single mom. The absence of Joseph in the adult life of Jesus suggests that Mary may have raised him and the rest of the kids alone. We need a simple home with a single mom and an ordinary laborer. Jesus' neighbors remembered him as a worker. "He's just a carpenter" (Mark 6:3 MSG).

Jesus had dirty hands, sweat-stained shirts, and—this may

surprise you—common looks. "No stately form or majesty that we should look upon Him, nor appearance that we should be attracted to Him" (Isaiah 53:2).

Drop-dead smile? Steal-your-breath physique? No. Heads didn't turn when Jesus passed. If he was anything like his peers, he had a broad peasant's face, dark olive skin, short curly hair, and a prominent nose. And, because people were smaller then, he was probably only about five feet tall. Hardly worthy of a *Teen People* cover.

Are your looks run-of-the-mill and your ways simple? So were his. He's been there.

Questionable pedigree. Raised in an overlooked nation among oppressed people in an obscure village. Simple home. Single mom. An ordinary laborer with ordinary looks. Can you spot him? See the adobe house with the thatched roof? Yes, the one with the chickens in the yard and the gangly teenager repairing chairs in the shed. Word has it he can fix your plumbing as well.

He's been there.

From the moment she glided gracefully into their shared room, Lindsey lived up to every one of Jane's expectations. *Oh, my, she is perfect!* And it was all downhill from there. Not that Lindsey seemed to notice. At least not at first.

"Jane!" Lindsey beamed, her amazing turquoise eyes alight with friendly interest. "It's so good to see you. Three whole days to really get to know each other; isn't it great?!"

"Uhh—" said Jane.

"Oh, the Mom Letters are fine for *facts*," Lindsey swept on, "but that's not the same as really *talking*, is it?"

"Umm—" said Jane.

"So tell me, wasn't it a hoot when . . ." And Lindsey was off and running, her musical voice filling the room with light-hearted chatter as she unpacked.

Overwhelmed by the nonstop flow of words, Jane couldn't think of a thing to say. Besides, what *do* you say to a tall, gorgeous "class president, soccer star, dancer" who models in her spare time and plans to be a brain surgeon?! Not that Lindsey mentioned any of those things. In fact—and this *did* surprise Jane—Lindsey's focus seemed to be on other people rather than herself. She seemed truly interested in Jane, too.

But by the time any of this registered with Jane, Lindsey all at once stopped talking—right in the middle of a sentence.

Oh, no, thought Jane, *I've messed up again! She really wants to be friends, and I'm not even trying!*

"Oh, no," said Lindsey, "I've messed up again! Talked way too fast about things you're probably not even interested in."

It never occurred to Jane that Lindsey, too, might be a little nervous about this meeting. "Well," managed a stunned Jane, "at least you've got things to talk *about*, and you do it without putting your foot in your mouth every time you open it."

Lindsey gave her small, quiet cousin a thoughtful look. Then she grinned. "No room for my foot with all those words in my mouth. Besides, what would it matter if I *did* say—or do— the wrong thing?"

Jane shrugged, as if the whole subject of embarrassing

goofs—not to mention a total lack of talent or achievement—didn't matter at all. "Oh, you wouldn't understand."

"Wouldn't I?" said Lindsey. "You might be surprised. Try me; I'll bet I've been there."

�֍ �֍ �֍   Jesus has been there.

"He had to enter into every detail of human life. Then, when he came before God as high priest to get rid of the people's sins, he would have already experienced it all himself—all the pain, all the testing—and would be able to help where help was needed" (Hebrews 2:17–18 MSG).

Jesus has been there.

Are you poor? Jesus knows how you feel. Are you on the lowest rung of the social ladder? He understands. Ever feel taken advantage of? Christ paid taxes to a foreign emperor.

He's been there. He understands the meaning of obscurity.

But what if your life is not obscure? What if you have a club to run or a team to manage or a class to lead? Can Jesus relate?

Absolutely. Jesus recruited and oversaw his own organization. Seventy men plus an assortment of women looked to him for leadership. Jesus understands the stress of leadership. His group included a zealot who hated the Romans and a tax collector who had worked for them.

Ever feel that you need to get away? So did Jesus. "Early the next morning, while it was still dark, Jesus woke and left the house. He went to a lonely place, where he prayed" (Mark 1:35 NCV).

Do you have too many activities to do in a day? Christ has been there. "Great crowds came to Jesus, bringing with them the lame, the blind, the crippled, those who could not speak, and many others. They put them at Jesus' feet, and he healed them" (Matthew 15:30 NCV).

How about family tensions? He's been there, too. "When his family heard what was happening, they tried to take him home with them. 'He's out of his mind,' they said" (Mark 3:21 NLT).

Have you been falsely accused? Jesus has. Enemies called Jesus a wino and a chowhound (Matthew 11:19).

Do your friends ever let you down? When Christ needed help, his friends dozed off. "You men could not stay awake with me for one hour?" (Matthew 26:40 NCV).

Unsure of the future? Jesus was. Regarding the last day of history, he explained, "No one knows when that day or time will be, not the angels in the heaven, not even the Son" (Matthew 24:36 NCV). Can Jesus be the Son of God and not know something? He can if he chooses not to. Knowing you would face the unknown, he chose to face the same.

Why would heaven's finest Son endure earth's toughest pain?

Jesus has been there. He was angry enough to purge the temple, hungry enough to eat raw grain, distraught enough to weep in public, playful enough to attract kids, weary enough to sleep in a storm-bounced boat, poor enough to sleep on dirt and borrow a coin for a sermon illustration, radical enough to get kicked out of town, responsible enough to care for his mother, tempted enough to know the smell of Satan, and fearful enough to sweat blood.

But why? Why would heaven's finest Son endure earth's toughest pain? So you would know that "He is able . . . to run to the cry of . . . those who are being tempted and tested and tried" (Hebrews 2:18 AMP).

Whatever you are facing, Jesus knows how you feel.

"Might as well face it, Jane," said Lindsey with a grin, "everybody messes up. The Carlton name comes with no guarantee of perfection. I should know!"

Lindsey's instinct to help—one of her finest qualities—was on full alert after very little time with the cousin who seemed so worried about messing up or looking silly. *Amazing*, thought Lindsey, *Jane has no idea how special she really is.*

"Tell me, Jane, did any of the Mom Letters mention the time I—" And Lindsey launched into a chronicle of hilarious misadventures.

The time Lindsey-the-Ballerina spun across the stage to leap gracefully into her partner's arms—and missed, crashing into the scenery. (Jane's lips twitched.) The time Lindsey-the-Class-President was introducing a visiting senator to a school assembly—and forgot his name. (Jane snorted.) The time Lindsey-the- Soccer-Star made a brilliant run downfield to execute a spectacular kick—into the *other* team's goal. (Jane cracked up.)

"Oh, my," said Jane, giving in to the giggles, "what did you *do?*"

"Oh," said Lindsey, as if it were totally obvious, "I just went on."

"But wasn't it . . . embarrassing?" Jane—who often felt like a drab duckling misplaced in a family of swans—was supersensitive about anything that made her look even *more* out of place.

"Embarrassing? Well, sure," said Lindsey, "but funny, too. Besides, people see what you show them. So . . ."

"So?" prompted Jane.

"So," explained Lindsey, "I just showed them something *other* than a disaster." She could see Jane was having trouble getting the picture. "Like . . . like that scenery I knocked over. I just picked it up and danced it back into place—you should have seen my partner's face! And the senator? I introduced him—and I quote—as 'a man who *needs* no introduction.' Gotta admit, the soccer thing was a little harder. The other kids never really bought into my theory about how a *really* good sport sometimes helps the other team, too!"

Jane couldn't remember when she'd laughed so much. Who'd have dreamed that being with her accomplished, "perfect" cousin would be so . . . comfortable?

The thing was, Jane had jumped to all the wrong conclusions about Lindsey—and, as it turned out, about herself, too.

What surprised Jane most of all was how much Lindsey seemed to know about *Jane's* very ordinary "accomplishments."

"What," said Lindsey, lifting an eyebrow, "you think *my* mom is the only one with bragging rights?"

"But there's nothing to brag about," protested Jane—who

didn't see nearly as much to admire in herself as others did. Well, sure, she made top grades. (But she had to work really hard for them.) And, yes, she did tons of volunteer work. (It wasn't always easy, but when someone needed help . . . you helped.) True, she did have a small talent for the piano. (But even with all her practice she'd never be concert quality—though the church and school choirs she played for didn't seem to mind.)

Really, there was nothing at all to fuss about. And none of it came easily. Not at all like the way the rest of her family seemed to float effortlessly from triumph to triumph.

"Aha!" exclaimed Lindsey. "There's your problem!"

"What?" asked a thoroughly confused Jane.

"You mean no one ever told you the Carlton Family Secret?!"

"Secret?"

Lindsey nodded, then leaned forward and whispered solemnly, "We just make it *look* easy. Actually, *no* one works harder than a Carlton!"

Jane's gray eyes opened very wide—as her point of view did a major switcheroo.

Maybe she wasn't so different after all! If hard work—however well-disguised—was the family standard, . . . well, Jane knew all about *that!* So, it seemed, did Lindsey. Who'd have dreamed?!

❊ ❊ ❊ Some time ago, twenty thousand of us ran through the streets of San Antonio, raising money for breast cancer research. Most of us ran out of kindness, happy to log three miles and donate a few dollars to the cause. A few ran in memory of loved ones, others in honor of cancer survivors. We ran for different reasons. But no runner was more passionate than a woman I spotted. A bandanna covered her bald head, and dark circles shadowed her eyes. She had cancer. While we ran out of kindness, she ran out of conviction. She knows how cancer victims feel. She is a cancer victim. She's been there.

So has Jesus. "He is able . . . to run to the cry of . . . those who are being tempted and tested and tried."

When you turn to him *for* help, he runs to you *to* help. Why? He knows how you feel. He's been there.

Jane hugged Lindsey good-bye. *Imagine, dreading something that turned out to be so fantastic!* Jane had not only found Lindsey to be entirely different than she'd expected, she'd also—thanks to Lindsey—been introduced to a whole new *Jane!* And *that* Jane fit very nicely, thank you, into this busy, confusing—exciting!—family of hers. And guess what? She always had.

And in the fall, Jane and Lindsey planned to get together for their own reunion!

"Oh, and Jane," whispered Lindsey, "about those Mom Letters? They'll be nothing compared to the new Jane/Lindsey E-Letters!"

"Right," said Jane with an answering grin.

Families! What could be more . . . wonderful?!

❊ ❊ ❊ By the way, remember how Jesus was not reluctant to call his ancestors his family? He's not ashamed of you, either: "Jesus, who makes people holy, and those who are made holy are from the same family. So he is not ashamed to call them his brothers and sisters" (Hebrews 2:11 NCV).

He's not ashamed of you. Nor is he confused by you. Your actions don't bewilder him. Your tilted halo doesn't trouble him. So go to him. After all, you're a part of his family.

friend of outcasts
(shady people)

matthew 9:9-13

> *As Jesus went on from there, He saw a man called Matthew,*
> *sitting in the tax collector's booth; and He said to him,*
> *"Follow Me!" And he got up and followed Him.*
>
> —Matthew 9:9

✳ ✳ ✳ "As Jesus was going down the road, he saw Matthew sitting at his tax-collection booth. 'Come, be my disciple,' Jesus said to him. So Matthew got up and followed him" (Matthew 9:9 NLT).

The surprise in this invitation is the one invited—a tax collector. Combine the greed of an embezzling executive with the attitude of a hokey television evangelist. Throw in the nerve of an ambulance-chasing lawyer and the cowardice of a drive-by sniper. Stir in a pinch of a thief's morality, and finish it off with a drug-peddler's code of ethics—and what do you have?

A first-century tax collector.

According to the Jews, these guys ranked barely above plankton on the food chain. Caesar permitted these Jewish citizens to tax almost anything—your boat, the fish you caught, your house, your crops. As long as Caesar got his due, they could keep the rest.

Matthew was a *public* tax collector. Private tax collectors hired other people to do the dirty work. Public publicans, like Matthew, just pulled their stretch limos into the poor side of town and set up shop. As crooked as corkscrews.

His given name was Levi, a priestly name (Mark 2:14; Luke 5:27–28). Did his parents aspire for him to enter the priesthood? If so, he was a big disappointment in the family circle.

You can bet he was shunned. The neighborhood cookouts? Never invited. High-school reunions? Somehow his name was left off the list. The guy was avoided like smallpox. Everybody kept his distance from Matthew.

Everyone except Jesus.

Brad could never quite figure out what had gone wrong—why people had begun avoiding him. *It started out just fine . . . I know they were impressed!*

When he'd first made his entrance—and it was definitely an Entrance-with-a-capital-*E*!—at Lincoln Middle School, Brad had been the immediate center of attention. Just as he'd planned. *Okay, maybe the sunshades and sequined vest* were *a little much. But, hey, when you're out to make an impression . . . make an impression!* And, indeed, he had.

The way Brad figured it, leaving everything he loved to move halfway across the country was tough enough . . . without going unnoticed when he got there. So he pulled out all the stops and played it to the hilt. LA "Cool" met Middle America—with a vengeance!

And it worked. From day one, everyone knew he'd arrived. How could they not? He was new. He was exotic. He was impossible to ignore. And the other kids were duly dazzled, awed, and fascinated by the outgoing, smooth-talking newcomer with the big ideas . . . at first.

> **If a little was good, he figured, a lot was better.**

Brad swam with the "big fish" at his old school, so that was the group he zeroed in on here, too. What he'd overlooked was that this was an entirely different pond. Back home—in his fast-paced West Coast world—trends, attitudes, *and* people came and went in the blink of an eye. To keep up you had to speak up, move fast . . . and worry about the details later. At Lincoln, life moved at a much less frantic pace.

Almost everybody had known almost everybody else since kindergarten. And the kids pretty much knew what to expect from one another. That's not to say they weren't intrigued by Brad's novelty.

Unfortunately, Brad *also* had a tendency to get carried away. If a little was good, he figured, a lot was better. So he talked too fast. Promised too much. Followed through too little. And, yes, exaggerated a little, here and there. As a result, the things he *really* had to offer—interesting ideas, an offbeat sense of humor, outstanding musical talent—were lost behind the glitter and flash.

It wasn't long, in fact, before Brad's outrageous stories and outlandish schemes started to come across to his classmates as bogus and self-serving. And Brad began to strike them as just a little too . . . *slick.* So they backed off. Of course, that just made Brad try all the harder. But the more he pushed, the more they retreated. By midyear, the kids whose lead most everyone else followed were keeping quite a distance between themselves and Brad. Which made it all the more surprising when Adam Greenwood did *not.*

✳ ✳ ✳ While everyone else avoided Matthew, Jesus had another approach to this shunned tax collector. "'Come, be my disciple,' Jesus said to him. So Matthew got up and followed him" (Matthew 9:9 NLT).

Matthew must have been ripe. Jesus hardly had to tug. Within a punctuation mark, Matthew's shady friends and Jesus' green followers are swapping e-mail addresses. "Then Levi gave a big dinner for Jesus at his house. Many tax collectors and other people were eating there, too" (Luke 5:29 NCV).

What do you suppose led up to that party? Let's try to imagine. I can see Matthew going back to his office and packing up. He removes the Collaborator of the Year Award from the wall and boxes up the Shady Business School certificate. His coworkers start asking questions.

"What's up, Matt? Headed on a cruise?"

"Hey, Matthew, the missus kick you out?"

Matthew doesn't know what to say. He mumbles something about a job change. But as he reaches the door, he pauses. Holding his box full of office supplies, he looks back. They're giving him hangdog looks—kind of sad, puzzled.

He feels a lump in his throat. Oh, these guys aren't much. Parents warn their kids about this sort. Salty language. Questionable morals. All kinds of bad habits. But a friend is a friend. Yet what can he do? Invite them to meet Jesus? Yeah, right. Preachers are *not* their thing. Tell them to tune in to the religious channel on TV? Then they'd think cotton-candy hair is a requirement for following Christ. What if he snuck little Torah tracts into their desks? Nah, they don't read.

So, not knowing what else to do, he shrugs his shoulders and gives them a nod. "These stupid allergies," he says, rubbing the mist from one eye.

Later that day the same thing happens. He goes to the bar to settle up his account. The decor is blue-collar chic: a seedy, smoky place with a pool table in the middle and a jukebox in the corner. Not the country club, but for Matthew, it's his home on the way home. And when he tells the owner he's moving on, the bartender responds, "Whoa, Matt. What's comin' down?"

Matthew mumbles an excuse about a job transfer but leaves with an empty feeling inside.

Later on he meets up with Jesus at a diner and shares his problem. "It's my buddies—you know, the guys at the office. And the fellows at the bar."

"What about them?" Jesus asks.

"Well, we kinda run together, you know. I'm gonna miss 'em. Take Josh, for instance—a real slick operator, but he visits orphans on Sunday. And Bruno at the gym? Can crunch you like a roach, but I've never had a better friend. He's posted bail for me three times."

Jesus motions for him to go on. "What's the problem?"

"Well, I'm gonna miss those guys. I mean, I've got nothing against Peter and James and John, Jesus . . . but they're Sunday morning, and I'm Saturday night. I've got my own circle, ya know?"

Jesus starts to smile and shakes his head. "Matthew, Matthew, you think I came to quarantine you? Following me doesn't mean forgetting your friends. Just the opposite. I want to meet them."

"Are you serious?"

"Is the high priest a Jew?"

"But, Jesus, these guys . . . half of them are on parole. Josh hasn't worn socks since his Bar Mitzvah. . . ."

"I'm not talking about a religious service, Matthew. Let me ask you—what do you like to do? Bowl? Play Monopoly? How's your golf game?"

Matthew's eyes brighten. "You ought to see me cook. I get on steaks like a whale on Jonah."

"Perfect." Jesus smiles. "Then throw a little going-away party. A hang-up-the-clipboard bash. Get the gang together."

Matthew's all over it. Calling the caterer, his housekeeper, his secretary. "Get the word out, Thelma. Cookout at my house tonight. Tell the guys to come and bring a date."

When Adam got the news, he was excited, a little nervous—and face-to-face with an opportunity. Being elected chairman of the Great Eight Gala was no small honor—and no small challenge.

It was a tradition at Lincoln Middle School that each year's graduating eighth graders left their school a special gift to remember them by. Over the years, Lincoln kids had come up with all kinds of ways to raise money for everything from an enormous school banner . . . to a fabulous trophy case (that had been a *really* good year, financially speaking).

Adam's class had already set their sights on a new sound system for the auditorium (which certainly needed one). All that remained was the slight detail of raising enough money.

As Gala chairman, Adam's first job was to choose the leadership team that would plan and organize the fund-raiser—*and* come up with the Big Idea. Then the entire class—the Ins, the Outs, the In-betweens—would work as one to make it happen. That was a Lincoln tradition, too—and something Adam thought should happen a lot more often. He'd never been comfortable with the way people seemed to gravitate to their own little groups—never considering what they missed by shutting out everyone else. But that was a concern for another time. Right now he had to get his committee chosen.

Karen, the Queen of Organized, was a natural choice. That girl could probably *herd cats!* Steve—who no doubt still had his first Tooth Fairy quarter—had the perfect sharp eye for keeping expenses down and profits up. Kim and Libby were natural "spark plugs"—overflowing with contagious enthusiasm. Throw in Todd's legendary determination, and Adam had the makings of a great team. With one addition. Someone who threw off ideas like July Fourth fireworks. Someone whose selection was going to raise quite a few eyebrows. Someone like . . . Brad.

Adam had thought for some time that everyone—including himself—had decided about Brad way too quickly. Yes, he talked too much, some of his stories *were* pretty far "out there," and the kids he was hanging out with now were kind of . . . questionable. But then Adam didn't really know *them* either, any more than he had known Brad—until they ended up in the same language arts class, and next to each other in orchestra. That's when Adam started noticing things.

For a guy who seemed so fixated on *himself*, Brad's essays were filled with appreciation for all kinds of fascinating things. And how could you *not* admire someone who played guitar like Brad did? A pretty fair picker himself, Adam knew real talent when he saw it. And when Brad dialed down the bells and whistles—and simply *talked* about things he really cared about—Adam started seeing the *person* behind the brash "personality."

When Brad invited Adam to sit in now and then with the garage band he was putting together, Adam did. And enjoyed it—even though the kids, and the music, were not his usual fare. So it seemed perfectly natural to Adam to join Brad and his friends at lunch now and then, and say "Hi!" when they passed in the halls. No big deal—though it did draw a comment or two from Adam's friends. But those comments were nothing compared to the reaction he got when he announced his choices for the Great Eight Gala Committee.

"Brad?! But what on earth do you see in *him*, Adam?!"

"Possibilities," said Adam, smiling to himself. "You'll see."

✳ ✳ ✳ It's quite a sight, the night Jesus ends up at Matthew's house—a classy split-level with a view of the Sea of Galilee. Parked out front is everything from BMWs to Harleys to limos. And the crowd inside tells you this is anything but a clergy conference.

Earrings on the guys and tattoos on the girls. Music that rumbles teeth roots. And buzzing around in the middle of the group is Matthew, making more connections than an electrician. He hooks up Peter with the tax collectors' bowling league and Martha with the kitchen staff. Simon the Zealot meets a high-school debate partner. And Jesus? Beaming. What could be better? Sinners and saints in the same room, and no one's trying to determine who is which. But an hour or so into the evening the door opens, and an icy breeze blows in. "The Pharisees and the men who taught the law for the Pharisees began to complain to Jesus' followers, 'Why do you eat and drink with tax collectors and sinners?' (Luke 5:30 NCV).

Enter the religious police and their thin-lipped piety. Big black books under arms. Cheerful as prison guards. Clerical collars so tight the veins bulge. They like to grill, too. But not steaks.

Matthew is the first to feel the heat. "Some religious fellow you are," one says, practically pulling an eyebrow muscle. "Look at the people you hang out with."

Matthew doesn't know whether to get mad or get out. Before he has time to choose, Jesus intervenes, explaining that Matthew is right where he needs to be. "'Healthy people don't need a doctor—sick people do. I have come to call sinners to turn from their sins, not to spend my time with those who think they are already good enough'" (Luke 5:31–32 NLT).

Quite a story. Matthew goes from double-dealer to disciple. He throws a party that makes the religious right uptight, but Christ proud. The good guys look good, and the bad guys hit the road. Some story, indeed.

What do we do with it?

That depends on which side of the tax collector's table you find yourself. You and I are Matthew. Don't look at me that way. There's enough hustler in the best of us to qualify for Matthew's table. Maybe you've never taken taxes, but you've taken liberty with the truth, taken credit that wasn't yours, taken advantage of the weak. You and I? Matthew.

If you're still at the table, you receive an invitation. "Follow me." So what if you've got a questionable reputation? So did Matthew. You may end up writing your own gospel.

You don't have to be weird to follow Jesus.

If you've left the table, you receive some encouraging news. You don't have to be weird to follow Jesus. You don't have to stop liking your friends to follow him. Just the opposite. He'd like to meet them, too. Do you know how to grill a steak?

It may have involved an unlikely mix of ingredients, but the Great Eight Gala fund-raiser was a huge success—thanks in large part to Brad.

To the surprise of everyone on the committee, he'd had little to say at first. They'd *expected* him to just take over and talk them to death. Instead, he kept his mouth shut and his mind open, while the rest of the committee tossed around—and tossed out—idea after idea.

Finally, when he couldn't contain himself any longer: "Look," said Brad—who could never be accused of thinking *small*—"why limit ourselves to just one thing? We want people to come and spend money, right? And we want to do it without spending a fortune ourselves. Am I right or am I right?"

Everyone obligingly nodded.

"So," said Brad, warming up, "let's give them choices!"

Choices?

"*Irresistible* choices," clarified Brad. "My mom absolutely can't get past a yard sale, the bigger the better. My dad loves having a clean car, but hates waiting in line. Everybody has junk to get rid of. And who doesn't like to be entertained? So let's do it all . . . big time!"

And so the Great Eight Bodacious Yard Sale, Grand Prix Car Wash & Band Challenge was born. And flourished. And made lots of money.

Trading free labor for the privilege of hauling away their finds, the entire eighth grade swept through most every garage, attic, and basement in town—then turned their trash-to-treasure discoveries into the yard sale to end all yard sales.

Dads went through the *long* car-wash line two and three times—just to get extra turns at the auto race video games designed by the Computer Club. The Chocolate Extravaganza bake sale lured appetites *and* wallets. And Brad's garage band, Alien Invasion—resplendent in wraparound sunshades and sequined vests—played their hearts out throughout the day.

And the Band *Challenge?* Well, that was Brad's brightest idea—and the one his admiring classmates found absolutely hilarious. For *two* dollars, Alien Invasion would play (or fake their way through) *any* request.

"Sometimes all they need is a chance."

And for *five* dollars, noise-weary adult ears could purchase five minutes of pure silence! Which many did. In fact, paying the band *not* to play turned out to be one of the biggest moneymakers of the day. And if a desire for silence didn't do the trick, it was amazing how quickly the band's talented performance could dissolve into discord. Accidentally, of course.

"Imagine that," said Brad in mock surprise as the still-chuckling committee counted the over-the-top proceeds of the day, "silence really *is* golden! Who'd have guessed?!"

"Who'd have guessed a *lot* of surprising things," agreed Adam with a grin, "or that sometimes all they need is a chance."

✳ ✳ ✳ Some time ago I was asked to play a game of golf. The foursome included two preachers, a church leader, and a "Matthew." The thought of four hours with three Christians, two of whom were preachers, did not appeal to him. His best friend, a Christ follower and his boss, insisted, so he agreed. I'm happy to report that he proclaimed the experience painless. On the ninth hole he turned to one of us and said, smiling, "I'm so glad you guys are normal." I think he meant this: "I'm glad you didn't get in my face or club me with a King James driver. Thanks for laughing at my jokes and telling a few yourself. Thanks for being normal." We didn't lower standards. But neither did we saddle a high horse. We were nice. Normal and nice.

Discipleship is sometimes defined by being normal.

A woman in a small Arkansas community was a single mom with a frail baby. Her neighbor would stop by every few days and keep the child so the mom could shop. After some weeks her neighbor shared more than time; she shared her faith, and the woman did what Matthew did. She followed Christ.

The friends of the young mother objected. "Do you know what those people teach?" they argued.

"Here is what I know," she told them. "They held my baby."

I think Jesus likes that kind of answer, don't you?

The next day he saw Jesus coming to him and said, "Behold, the Lamb of God who takes away the sin of the world!"

—John 1:29

Okay, that's it! I can't go another step—not with this load.

With all the drama at a thirteen-year-old diva's command, Cassie heaved a sigh . . . flung off her bulging daypack . . . and collapsed onto a convenient trail-side rock. Unfortunately, she was performing for an audience of one—herself. The rest of her hiking group was out of sight around the next bend in the trail. There was only Cassie . . . and her burden.

I can't go another step—not with this load.

❊ ❊ ❊ The woman flops down on the bench and drops a trash bag between her feet. With elbows on knees and cheeks in hands, she stares at the sidewalk. Everything aches. Back. Legs. Neck. Her shoulder is stiff and her hands raw. All because of the sack.

Oh, to be rid of this garbage.

Oh, to be rid of this garbage.

Unbroken clouds form a gray ceiling, gray with a thousand sorrows. Soot-stained buildings cast long shadows, darkening passageways and the people in them. Drizzle chills the air and muddies the rivulets of the street gutters. The woman collects her jacket. A passing car drenches the sack and splashes her jeans. She doesn't move. Too tired.

Her memories of life without the trash are fuzzy. As a child maybe? Her back was straighter, her walk quicker . . . or was it a dream? She doesn't know for sure.

A second car. This one stops and parks. A man steps out. She watches his shoes sink in the slush. From the car he pulls out a trash bag, lumpy with litter. He drapes it over his shoulder and grumbles at the weight.

Neither of them speaks. Who knows if he noticed her. His face seems young, younger than his stooped back. In moments he is gone. Her gaze returns to the pavement.

She never looks at her trash. Early on she did. But what she saw repulsed her, so she's kept the sack closed ever since.

What else can she do? Give it to someone? All have their own.

Here comes a young mother. With one hand she leads a child, with the other she drags her load, bumpy and heavy.

Here comes an old man, face ravined with wrinkles. His trash sack is so long it hits the back of his legs as he walks. He glances at the woman and tries to smile.

What weight would he be carrying? she wonders as he passes.

"Regrets."

She turns to see who spoke. Beside her on the bench sits a man. Tall, with angular cheeks and bright, kind eyes. Like hers, his jeans are mud-stained. Unlike hers, his shoulders are straight. He wears a T-shirt and baseball cap. She looks around for his trash but doesn't see it. *Strange. Everyone else is loaded down with trash. Why isn't he? What's his secret?*

What's their secret—why are things so easy for other people, and so hard for me?!

Nudging a stray pine cone with the toe of her dusty hiking boot, Cassie glared at her way-too-full daypack—as if it had somehow packed *itself* with all the must-haves, can't-do-with-outs, and might-needs Cassie had insisted on bringing. The other kids—and Maggie, their counselor—had tried to warn her. "Way too much stuff." "Better leave some behind." "It's only a *day* hike, Cassie."

As she'd lagged farther and farther behind—*And no one even missed her!*—it became clear they were right: *She definitely needed a Sherpa!* (Although the chances were slim that one of the sturdy Himalayan porters would show up *here*, on the trail to Overlook Point.)

The problem was, Cassie was very attached to her "stuff"—so she carried it with her everywhere she went, whether she needed it or not, just in case.

Unfortunately, it wasn't just material things Cassie had trouble leaving behind. No one could hold on to a hurt, imagined slight, worry, or the past more fiercely than Cassie could. In fact, it was her talent for clinging to things she'd be better off without that held her back from a lot of *other* things—including the kind of friendships she'd wanted.

It's not as if I don't try! But people just don't seem to like me. It never occurred to Cassie that the baggage from the past she dragged along each time might be what made friendship such an uphill climb. (Kind of like that humongous daypack that was holding her back on today's hike.)

Cassie had never learned to travel light—which was turning out to be quite a problem. And how can you get *past* your problems when you insist on carrying them with you?

✳ ✳ ✳ Forgetting her own troubles for a moment, the woman stares at the stranger beside her on the bench. "What do you mean, 'regrets'?" she asks him. He watches the old man trudge away with his bag as he explains, "As a young father, he worked many hours and neglected his family. His children don't love him. His sack is full—full of regrets."

She doesn't respond. And when she doesn't, he does.

"And yours?"

"Mine?" she asks, looking at him . . . and carefully *not* looking at the bulging sack between her feet.

"Shame." His voice is gentle, compassionate.

She still doesn't speak, but neither does she turn away.

"Too many hours in the wrong places, with the wrong people. Last year. Last night . . . shame."

She stiffens, steeling herself against the scorn she has learned to expect. As if she needed more shame. Stop him. But how? She awaits his judgment.

But it never comes. His voice is warm and his question honest: "Will you give me your trash?"

Her head draws back. *What can he mean?*

"Give it to me. Tomorrow. At the landfill. Will you bring it?" He rubs a moist smudge from her cheek with his thumb and stands. "Friday. The landfill."

Long after he leaves, she sits, replaying the scene, retouching her cheek. His voice lingers; his invitation hovers. She tries to dismiss his words but can't. How could he know what he knew? And how could he know and still be so kind? The memory sits on the couch of her soul, an uninvited but welcome guest.

That night's sleep brings her summer dreams. A young girl under blue skies and puffy clouds, playing amid wildflowers, skirt twirling. She dreams of running with hands wide open, brushing the tops of sunflowers. She dreams of happy people filling a meadow with laughter and hope.

But when she wakes, the sky is dark, the clouds billow, and the streets are shadowed. At the foot of her bed lies her sack of trash. Hoisting it over her shoulder, she walks out of the apartment and down the stairs and onto the street, still slushy.

It's Friday.

For a time she stands, thinking. First wondering what he meant, then if he really meant it. She sighs. With hope just barely outweighing hopelessness, she turns toward the edge of town. Others are walking in the same direction. The man beside her smells of alcohol. He's slept many nights in his suit. A teenage girl walks a few feet ahead. The woman of shame hurries to catch up. The girl volunteers an answer before the question can be asked: "Rage. Rage at my father. Rage at my mother. I'm tired of anger. He said he'd take it." She motions to her sack. "I'm going to give it to him."

The woman nods, and the two walk together.

A group hike isn't much fun when you're walking alone. And—as she jumped up, hoisted her pack, and started trudging up the trail—Cassie was definitely alone. Very alone. In a suddenly way-too-*quiet* forest.

It was the silence, in fact, that had roused Cassie from her thoughts . . . and her rock. She'd meant to rest only a few minutes, then catch up with the rest of the kids she could hear chattering just around the next bend. But time had slipped away as she brooded about the morning's frustrations: The advice about carrying too much, which Cassie heard as criticism. Ella's and Heather's giggles, which Cassie was positive were about *her*. The way she'd had to sit by herself on the bus, never mind that her overflowing pack left room for no one else.

Just as Cassie was working up to a really good session of

"Poor Me," she suddenly realized that she couldn't hear the other kids at all. *Uh-oh! I'd better get moving.* But that was easier *said* than done.

By the time she'd struggled fifty feet *up* the trail—with the weight of her pack pulling her back *down* the trail—she had to admit the kids were right. *It is too heavy! I've got to lighten my load. But how?* (Though she already knew.)

Cassie dropped her pack smack in the middle of the trail, knelt beside it . . . and took inventory. Did she really need *five* extra pairs of socks? A sweatshirt *and* a windbreaker? In June?! Toothbrush, mouthwash, nail polish . . . *nail polish?!* Soap and towel . . . *Really, Cassie! A little dirt never hurt anybody. And* two *paperbacks?!*

Reluctantly, Cassie sorted her things into three piles: Must-haves. Like-to-keeps. Can-live-withouts . . . barely.

Her compass, map, and pocketknife were definite keepers. Bandages and moleskin, yes; but the rest of her three-pound first-aid kit would have to go. Binoculars? Absolutely. So she hung them around her neck, along with her new camera. But maybe five rolls of film *were* a little much.

Okay, making real progress here, Cassie encouraged herself. There still remained, however, the issue of munchies—three apples, one squashed banana, four just-in-case energy bars, a lone chocolate bar, *and* her actual lunch. Shaking the nearly full canteen on her belt, Cassie decided maybe five extra bottles of water *were* just a tad . . . excessive.

Now for the hard part . . . With a sigh, Cassie slowly moved most of her like-to-keep pile over to the discard stack. That left just one problem: what to do with it all. Littering was out of the question, of course—especially in such a gorgeous wilderness area. So it was time to improvise.

A depression in a rock filled with her "backup" water made a handy drinking bowl—and cut-up apples and energy bars, an impromptu feast—for any critters that might wander by. (She ate the chocolate herself.) But what was she going to do with the nonedible stuff? *Wait a minute, isn't that*—Yes! Up ahead, just where the trail curved again, she spotted a Forest Service trash barrel. Perfect! Sort of.

It took three trips for Cassie to carry all her "stuff" to the barrel. Parting with it wasn't easy, but she had no choice. She really *didn't* need it—and it was just holding her back from where she wanted to go. That was when it struck her: *I wonder what* else *I've been dragging along with me that's just getting in my way?!* And she wasn't thinking about material things—though an overflowing trash barrel *was* a rather strange place for a flash of enlightenment.

❊ ❊ ❊ The landfill is tall with trash—papers and broken brooms and old beds and rusty cars. By the time they reach the hill, the line to the top is long. Hundreds walk ahead of them. All wait in silence, stunned by what they hear—a scream, a pain-pierced roar that hangs in the air for moments, interrupted only by a groan. Then the scream again.

His.

As they draw nearer, they know why. He kneels before each person who comes, gesturing toward the sack, offering a request, then a prayer. "May I have it? And may you never feel it again." Then he bows his head and lifts the sack, emptying its contents upon himself. The selfishness of the glutton, the bitterness of the angry, the possessiveness of the insecure. He feels what they felt. It is as if he'd lied or cheated or cursed his Maker.

> **"May I have it? And may you never feel it again."**

Upon her turn, the woman pauses. Hesitates. His eyes compel her to step forward. He reaches for her trash and takes it from her. "You can't live with this," he explains. "You weren't made to." With head down, he empties her shame upon his shoulders. Then looking toward the heavens with tear-flooded eyes, he screams, "I'm sorry!"

"But you did nothing!" she cries.

Still, he sobs as she has sobbed into her pillow a hundred nights. That's when she realizes that his cry is hers. Her shame his.

With her thumb she touches his cheek, and for the first step in a long nighttime, she has no trash to carry.

Cassie stood by the filled-to-the-top trash barrel feeling curiously light and . . . free. Without the load she'd been carrying, she'd practically be able to *fly* the rest of the way to the top! But, oh, it was hard—leaving behind the things she'd been attached to for so long.

She looked down at the CD player she still held. Should she? *Must* she? But before she could make up her mind . . .

"Cassie! *There* you are," called Heather, coming back down the trail.

"My goodness," added Ella, "we thought you'd been carried off by Big Foot!"

They came back for me! "Oh," said Cassie, moving to hide the trash barrel, "I was just taking my time."

"Right," said Heather.

"Sure," said Ella. And they looked at each other and grinned.

Oh, great! thought Cassie, *they'll have a lot of fun with* this *story!* "Wh—what are you doing here?"

And that was when they surprised her.

"Well," said Heather, stepping around Cassie to look into the trash barrel, "we thought maybe you could use a hand."

"And we were right!" added Ella, rummaging around in Cassie's discards. "Cassie! This is your favorite sweatshirt. You can't leave *that!*" And Ella tied the shirt around her own waist.

"Or this," added Heather, taking the CD player from Cassie and tucking it into her own pack. "If you want, we'll carry some things for you. A *few* things," she added quickly.

"But . . . but why would you do that? You don't even like me!"

Heather looked at Ella. Ella looked at Heather. "Actually—" began Heather, "we thought *you* didn't like *us*," finished Ella.

"But," said a puzzled Cassie, "you came back to help anyway?"

"Well, sure," said Heather, "why wouldn't we?"

"After all," added Ella, "we might have been mistaken."

"Oh," said Cassie. Then, "Thanks, you guys. I won't forget

this." And she didn't. Not ever. After all, there are some things *worth* hanging on to—and they don't weigh you down at all. In fact they can be positively . . . uplifting—like the view from Overlook Point that the girls now shared together.

✤ ✤ ✤ With the others the woman stands at the base of the hill and watches as the selfless stranger is buried under a mound of misery. For some time he moans. Then nothing. Just silence.

The people sit among the wrecked cars and papers and discarded stoves and wonder who this man is and what he has done. Like mourners at a wake, they linger. Some share stories. Others say nothing. All cast occasional glances at the landfill. It feels odd, loitering near the heap. But it feels even stranger to think of leaving.

So they stay. Through the night and into the next day. Darkness comes again. A kinship connects them, a kinship through the trashman. Some doze. Others build fires in the metal drums and speak of the sudden abundance of stars in the night sky. By early morning most are asleep.

They almost miss the moment. It is the young girl who sees it. The girl with the rage. She doesn't trust her eyes at first, but when she looks again, she knows.

Her words are soft, intended for no one. "He's standing."

Then aloud, for her friend, "He's standing."

And louder for all, "He's standing!"

She turns; all turn. They see him silhouetted against a golden sun.

Standing. Indeed.

CHAPTER 5

TRY AGAIN
(DISCOURAGED PEOPLE)

LUKE 5:1-11

Simon answered and said, "Master, we worked hard all night and caught nothing, but I will do as You say and let down the nets."

—Luke 5:5

❊ ❊ ❊ There is a look that says, "It's too late." You've seen it. The rolling of the eyes, the shaking of the head, the pursing of the lips.

Your parents are talking divorce. "Can't you try one more time?" you beg.

"Sorry, sweetheart," they say, "we've already done that."

Your two closest friends aren't speaking to one another. Haven't for weeks. "Won't you try again?" you ask one of them. She looks away, inhales deeply, and sighs.

Your older brother has always dreamed of going to one

particular college. Earlier this year he got very sick and missed months of school. But he insists on taking the pre-SATs anyway. His scores are a disaster—nowhere near the standards of the college of his dreams. Your mom tries to make the best of it. "There's still time. You could take some summer classes. Or arrange for special tutoring. Maybe even consider other colleges." You might as well have told him to swim to London. He shakes his head. "I'll never catch up. . . . It's too late."

Too late to save a marriage.

Too late to mend a friendship.

Too late to save a dream.

Too late to catch any fish. Or so Peter thinks. All night he fished. He witnessed both the setting and the rising of the sun but has nothing to show for it. While other fishermen cleaned their catch, he just cleaned his nets. But now Jesus wants him to try again.

"Now it happened that while the crowd was pressing around Him and listening to the word of God, [Jesus] was standing by the lake of Gennesaret" (Luke 5:1).

In Jesus' time, the area around the Sea of Gennesaret, or Galilee, bustled with people. Nine of the seacoast villages boasted populations of fifteen thousand-plus. And you get the impression that a good portion of those people were present the morning Christ ministered on the beach. As more people arrived, more people pressed. With every press, Jesus took a step back. Soon he was stepping off the sand and into the water. That's when he had an idea.

He saw two boats lying at the edge of the lake; but the fishermen had gotten out of them and were washing their nets. And He got into one of the boats, which was Simon's, and asked him to put out a little way from the land. And he sat down and began teaching the people from the boat. When He had finished speaking, He said to Simon, "Put out into the deep water and let down your nets for a catch." (Luke 5:2–4)

Jesus needs a boat; Peter provides one. Jesus preaches; Peter is content to listen. Jesus suggests a midmorning fishing trip, however, and Peter gives him a look. The it's-too-late look. He runs his fingers through his hair and sighs. "Master, we worked hard all night and caught nothing" (Luke 5:5). Can you feel Peter's discouragement?

Discouraged? You *could* describe Chris that way. But, actually, words like *dejected, deflated, depressed,* and maybe even *defeated* come a lot closer to his mood.

And who could blame him? Losing a lifelong friendship *is* a downer of major proportions—especially when *you* are the one who sank the boat. Chris had tried everything he could think of to fix things, but Ryan wasn't buying any of it.

And who could blame him? Chris had pulled the rug out from under their friendship—and the fall hurt. A lot. Oh, they'd had their ups and downs over the years, but they'd always managed to work things out. This time, though, Ryan wasn't so sure they could . . . or even *should*.

Their friendship had been an amazement to everyone right

from the start. Boisterous, daredevil Chris and quiet, studious Ryan?! Go figure. As different as night and day, they somehow fit perfectly together.

If Chris was a kite pinwheeling through the air, Ryan was the steady hand on the string working the wind. If Ryan was the nose-to-the-grindstone who got things *finished*, Chris was the spark plug who got things *started*. Ryan would never have Chris's skill on a skateboard, but—with Chris's tips—he at least avoided breaking anything. Chris would never be a chess master, but—thanks to Ryan—he *could* tell a knight from a rook and had developed a real talent for strategy. And, of course, there was the fishing with Ryan's Grandpa Malone.

Grandpa Malone was the only one who *wasn't* puzzled by their friendship. "Who cares *why* it works as long as it does?" he'd say, then wink at the boys. "You guys ready for another try at catching Old Devious?" And the three of them would hook Grandpa's boat to his old pickup and head for the lake. Though, truth be told, over the years both boys *did* start to wonder if the giant—and oh-so-tricky—fish of Grandpa's stories really existed at all. Grandpa Malone would never say. He'd just grin and change the subject—and Grandpa *never* ran out of subjects!

Grandpa Malone had a funny story or off-the-wall opinion for any occasion. Oddly enough, many of them just *happened* to deal with quandaries the boys ran into over the years. Not that Grandpa *ever* gave advice. "Advice?" he'd snort. "Don't believe in it. The best answers are the ones we find for ourselves. That's why God gave us minds . . . and hearts."

I wonder what Grandpa Malone would say about this *mess?*

> ### The best answers are the ones we find for ourselves.

Actually—even though he was much too embarrassed to call Ryan's grandfather these days—Chris had a pretty good idea what he'd say: Grandpa would agree that he'd gotten himself into a real pickle. And what was Chris going to do about it?

That was the problem. Chris had tried everything he could think of to make things right with Ryan. But nothing worked. And he was out of ideas. Finding a solution was as frustrating as . . . as finding Old Devious!

�֍ �֍ �֍ All night Peter's boat floated fishless on the black sheet of the sea. Lanterns of distant vessels bounced like fireflies. The men swung their nets and filled the air with the rhythm of their trade.

Swish, slap . . . silence.

Swish, slap . . . silence.

Midnight.

Excited voices from across the lake reached the men. Another boat had found a school. Peter considered moving but decided against it.

Swish, slap . . . silence.

Two o'clock in the morning. Peter rested while his brother fished. Then Andrew rested. James, floating nearby, suggested a move. The others agreed. Wind billowed the sails and blew the boats to a cove. The rhythm resumed.

Swish, slap . . . silence.

Every yank of the net was easy. Too easy. No matter how hard the men worked, they caught nothing.

Golden shafts of light eventually reclaimed the sky. Most mornings the sunrise inspired the men. Today it only tired them. They didn't want to see it. Who wants to dock an empty boat? Who wants to tie up and clean up, knowing the first question the wife is going to ask? And, most of all, who wants to hear a well-rested carpenter-turned-rabbi say, "Put out into the deep water and let down your nets for a catch" (Luke 5:4)?

Oh, the thoughts Peter might have had. *I'm tired. Bone tired. I want a meal and a bed, not a fishing trip. Am I his tour guide? Besides, half of Galilee is watching. I feel like a loser already. Now he wants to put on a midmorning fishing exhibition? You can't catch fish in the morning. Count me out.*

Whatever thoughts Peter had were distilled to one phrase: "We worked hard all night and caught nothing" (Luke 5:5).

Do you have any worn, wet, empty nets? Do you know the feeling of a sleepless, fishless night? Of course you do. For what have you been casting?

Confidence? "I've worked so hard to be prepared, but every time I get up to speak in class I freeze. . . ."

Trust? "I know how my parents feel about lying, but somehow I just keep messing up. . . ."

Faith? "I want to believe, but . . ."

Friendship? "No matter what I do . . ."

I've worked hard all night and caught nothing.

You've felt what Peter felt. You've sat where Peter sat. And now Jesus is asking you to go fishing. He knows your nets are empty. He knows your heart is weary. He knows you'd like nothing more than to turn your back on the mess and just give up.

But he urges, "It's not too late to try again."

He knows your heart is weary.

See if Peter's reply won't help you with your own: "I will do as You say and let down the nets" (Luke 5:5).

Not much passion in those words. You might hope for a ten-thousand-candle smile and a fist pumping the air. "I got Jesus in my boat. Mama, warm up the oven!" But Peter shows no excitement. He feels none. Now he has to unfold the nets, pull out the oars, and convince James and John to postpone their rest. He has to work. If faith is measured in seeds, Peter is fresh out. Inspired? No. But obedient? Admirably. And a smidgen of obedience is all Jesus wants.

Things usually fell obediently into place for Chris. His optimistic attitude and happy-go-lucky spirit were hard to resist, and people just naturally found themselves seeing things his way. Even Ryan wasn't immune. Usually. Until things—a *lot* of things—changed.

The changes—which had started last fall, when Ryan and Chris moved up to high school—didn't seem like such a big deal at first. After all, high school *is* a time of change. New people to meet. New things to try. And Ryan and Chris had jumped right in—each in his own way.

Chris's outgoing personality and talent for athletics quickly attracted a group of like-minded spirits. Ryan gravitated to the Chess and Science Clubs. Chris tried out for soccer. Ryan joined the debate team. Chris ran for class president. Ryan ran for the library. All of which was fine. They still met up at lunch most every day; compared notes on most everything; and remained each other's biggest fans . . . at first.

As the months passed, however, their times together grew fewer and farther apart. Lunch dropped to two or three times a week, then once a week, then . . . well, almost never. After school? Weekends? Same story. Different friends and activities pulled them farther and farther apart. The problem was: Ryan tried to *do* something about the growing separation; Chris only *meant* to.

Then, a while back—though Ryan tried hard not to believe it—it started to seem as if Chris were almost . . . *ashamed* to be seen with him at all! But, *Nah, you're imagining things,* Ryan told himself. So, each time, Ryan would cut his busy friend just a little more slack.

But Chris used up the last of that slack two weeks ago in the cafeteria. Ryan had stopped by the noisy table—with Chris in the middle of hijinks as usual—just to say "Hi!" But when no one—including Chris—invited him to sit down, Ryan stood there a moment, then turned and walked away. Unfortunately, he didn't walk fast enough. He was still within earshot when he heard the question . . . *and* Chris's answer.

"Chris, my man, what's a cool dude like you see in such a . . . loser?"

"Uh . . . you know . . . we've lived next door for years. And, hey, he's not so bad."

He regretted the words the moment they left his mouth. But it was too late. And the hurt look on Ryan's face hit Chris like a bucket of ice water. *What am I doing?! He's my oldest friend, and I've just sliced him up into little pieces to look "cool" for my new friends. Talk about losers!*

If Chris could have eaten his words, he would have. But he couldn't. They were gone—past recall. So was Ryan. No matter what Chris had tried since—and he'd tried everything he could think of to show how sorry he was—Ryan was polite, pleasant . . . and not convinced. And now Chris was completely out of ideas. Even Grandpa Malone—when Chris swallowed his pride and called him—wasn't much help.

"I'm afraid it's too late, Grandpa. I've tried everything, but nothing seems to do any good."

"Too late, huh? Well, you know what they say, Chris. When you've tried everything, there's just one thing to do."

"What?" asked a hopeful Chris.

"Try *again*," came the answer. "You just never know when you might be surprised."

> ## "When you've tried everything, there's just one thing to do."

✳ ✳ ✳ Peter isn't a happy camper when Jesus asks him to take the boat out again that morning. But he is an obedient one. And that's all Jesus needs.

"Put out into the deep water," the God-man instructs.

Why the deep water? You suppose Jesus knew something Peter didn't?

You suppose Jesus is doing with Peter what parents do with their kids on Easter Sunday? They find most of the eggs on their own. But a couple of treasures inevitably survive the first harvest. "Look," I'd whisper in the ears of my daughters, "behind the tree." A quick search around the trunk, and, what do you know, Dad was right. Spotting treasures is easy for the one who hid them. Finding fish is simple for the God who made them. To Jesus, the Sea of Galilee is a dollar-store fishbowl on a kitchen cabinet.

Peter gives the net a swish, lets it slap, and watches it disappear. Luke doesn't tell us what Peter did while he was waiting for the net to sink, so I will. (I'm glancing heavenward for lightning.)

I like to think that Peter, while holding the net, looks over his shoulder at Jesus. And I like to think that Jesus, knowing Peter is about to be half-yanked into the water, starts to smile. A daddy-daughter-Easter-egg smile. His eyes crinkle up. A dash of white flashes beneath his whiskers. Jesus tries to hold it back but can't.

There is so much to smile about. It's Easter Sunday, and the lawn is crawling with kids. Just wait till they look under the tree.

When they had done this, they enclosed a great quantity of fish, and their nets began to break; so they signaled to their partners in the other boat for them to come and help them. And they came and filled both of the boats, so that they began to sink. (Luke 5:6–7)

Peter's arm is yanked into the water. It's all he can do to hang on until the other guys can help. Within moments the four fishermen and the carpenter are up to their knees in flopping silver.

Peter lifts his eyes off the catch and onto the face of Christ. In that moment, for the first time, he sees Jesus. Not Jesus the Fish Finder. Not Jesus the Multitude Magnet. Not Jesus the Rabbi. Peter sees Jesus the Lord.

Peter falls face-first among the fish. Their stink doesn't bother him. It is his stink that he's worried about. "Go away from me Lord, for I am a sinful man, O Lord!" (Luke 5:8).

Christ had no intention of honoring that request. He doesn't abandon self-confessed bunglers. Quite the contrary, he enlists them. "Do not fear, from now on you will be catching men" (Luke 5:10).

Contrary to what you may have been told, Jesus doesn't limit his recruiting to the stout-hearted. The beat-up and worn-out are prime prospects in his book, and he's been known to climb into boats and bars, gutters and garrets, prisons and palaces to tell them, "It's not too late to start over."

Peter learned the lesson. But wouldn't you know it? Peter forgot the lesson. Two short years later, this man who confessed Christ in the boat cursed Christ at a fire. The night before Jesus' crucifixion, Peter told people that he'd never heard of Jesus.

He couldn't have made a more tragic mistake. He knew it. The burly fisherman buried his bearded face in thick hands and spent Friday night in tears. All the feelings of that Galilean morning came back to him.

It's too late.

But then Sunday came. Jesus came! Peter saw him. Peter was

convinced that Christ had come back from the dead. But apparently Peter wasn't convinced that Christ came back for him.

So he went back to the boat—to the same boat, the same beach, the same sea. He came out of retirement. He and his buddies washed the barnacles off the hull, unpacked the nets, and pushed out. They fished all night, and, honest to Pete, they caught nothing.

Poor Peter. Blew it as a disciple. Now he's blowing it as a fisherman. About the time he wonders if it's too late to take up carpentry, the sky turns orange, and they hear a voice from the coastline. "Had any luck?"

They yell back, "No."

"Try the right side of the boat!"

With nothing to lose and no more pride to protect, they give it a go. "So they cast, and then they were not able to haul it in because of the great number of fish" (John 21:6). It takes a moment for the déjà vu to hit Peter. But when it does, he cannonballs into the water and swims as fast as he can to the One who loved him enough to *re-create* a miracle. This time the message stuck.

Peter never again fished for fish. He spent the rest of his days telling anyone who would listen, "It's not too late to try again."

Chris couldn't get Grandpa Malone's words out of his mind: "It's never too late to try again, Chris. 'Course, it works better if you're trying the *right* thing."

"The right thing?" asked Chris, hoping for some kind of "formula" that would mend his broken friendship with Ryan.

But Grandpa wasn't much help. "Oh, you'll know it when you see it," was all he'd say.

✳ ✳ ✳

"Yeah, right," Chris grumbled to himself the next day, "I'll know it when I see it." *So where is it? Unless . . . unless I've been looking in the wrong place!*

Next thing Chris knew, he was doing something he rarely ever did—some deep thinking. It was strange territory for Chris, who was more likely to bound lightheartedly over the *surface* of things than to ponder what might lie beneath. And, hey, his everything-will-work-out approach to life had always . . . worked. Until now. What was so different *this* time?

That's when it hit him: He'd expected things to fix *themselves* this time, too! And anyone with a brain would know that couldn't happen. He'd neglected the friendship too many times. His words of betrayal had been too hurtful. And all those "everythings" he'd tried to mend the friendship with? Well, they'd included everything *except* an actual apology!

No wonder Ryan isn't willing to just pick up where we left off! Who can blame him?

Chris's soul-searching had hit the nail right on the head. While Chris might be content to just skim the surface of things, Ryan's questing intelligence never quit until *he* reached the core of an issue. And what Ryan had sadly concluded was this:

Their friendship really didn't matter to Chris. And no easy words could change that truth. *Better to just let it go. Sure, it hurts. But, hey, grow up!*

Talk about timing! Just as Ryan accepted that their friendship doesn't matter all that much to Chris . . . *Chris* realized that nothing matters *more!* Which made their next conversation something of a surprise to them both.

"Uh . . . Ryan?" Silver-tongued Chris was stuck for words, but he forged ahead anyway. "Look. I've got something to say, and a question to ask. I wouldn't blame you if you didn't listen to either one. But I hope you will."

Ryan, kind of stuck for words himself, just nodded.

"I was wrong," said Chris. "What I said that day . . . I didn't mean it, and I know it really hurt you. I've never been sorrier about anything. I hope you can forgive me."

Ryan didn't know what to say, so he played for time. "Uh . . . and the question?"

"Oh, *that*," said Chris, not sure how things were going. "Is . . . is there still a place for me in Grandpa's boat?"

Ryan started to smile. "Still hoping to catch Old Devious?"

"No," said Chris, "I'm after much bigger game."

"Oh?" said Ryan.

"Yeah . . . my best friend . . . if it's not too late?" Chris held his breath.

Ryan thought it over. But not for long. He believed—now— that Chris really *was* sorry, and that their friendship *did* matter to him. And that was all he needed to know.

"How could it *ever* be too late . . . for friends?" asked Ryan.

❊ ❊ ❊ Is it too late for you to try again? Before you say yes, before you fold up the nets and head for the house—two questions. Have you given Christ your boat? Your heartache? Your dead-end dilemma? Your struggle? Have you really turned it over to him? And have you gone deep? Have you bypassed the surface-water solutions you can see, in search of the deep-channel provisions God can give? Try the other side of the boat. Go deeper than you've gone. You may find what Peter found. The payload of his second effort was not the fish he caught but the God he saw.

"Let's try again—this time with me on board."

The God-man who spots weary fishermen, who cares enough to enter their boats, who will turn his back on the adoration of a crowd to solve the frustration of a friend. The next door Savior who whispers this word to the owners of empty nets: "Let's try again—this time with me on board."

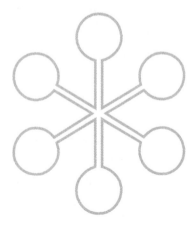

chapter 6

SPit THERAPY
(SUFFering PEOPLE)

JOHN 9:1-38

*Jesus heard that they had put him [the healed blind man] out,
and finding him, He said, "Do you believe in the Son of Man?"
He answered, "Who is He, Lord, that I may believe in Him?"
Jesus said to him, "You have both seen Him, and He is
the one who is talking with you."*

—John 9:35–37

❊ ❊ ❊ The old guy at the corner hasn't seen him. The woman selling the figs hasn't, either. Jesus describes him to the scribes at the gate and the kids in the courtyard. "He's about this tall. Clothes are ragged. Belly-length beard."

No one has a clue.

For the better part of a day, Jesus has been searching up and down the Jerusalem streets. He didn't stop for lunch. Hasn't paused to rest. The only time his feet aren't moving is when he is asking, "Pardon me, but have you seen the fellow who used to beg on the corner?"

He searched the horse stable and checked out the roof of a shed. Now Jesus is going door-to-door. "He has a homeless look," Jesus tells people. "Unkempt. Dirty. And he has muddy eyelids."

Finally, a boy gives him a lead. Jesus takes a back street toward the temple and spots the man sitting on a stump between two donkeys. Christ approaches from behind and places a hand on his shoulder. "There you are! I've been looking for you." The fellow turns and, for the first time, sees the One who let him see. And what the man does next you may find hard to believe.

But first let me catch you up. John introduces him to us with these words: "As [Jesus] passed by, He saw a man blind from birth" (John 9:1). This man has never seen a sunrise. Can't tell purple from pink. The disciples fault the family tree. "Rabbi, who sinned, this man or his parents, that he would be born blind?" (John 9:2).

Neither, the God-man replies. Trace this condition back to heaven. The reason the man was born sightless? So that "the works of God might be displayed in him" (John 9:3).

Talk about a thankless role. Selected to suffer. Some sing to God's glory. Others teach to God's glory. Who wants to be blind for God's glory? Which is tougher—the condition or discovering it was God's idea?

The cure proves to be as surprising as the cause. "[Jesus] spat on the ground, and made clay of the spittle, and applied the clay to his eyes" (John 9:6).

The world abounds with paintings of the God-man: in the

arms of Mary, in the Garden of Gethsemane, in the Upper Room, in the darkened tomb. Jesus touching. Jesus weeping, laughing, teaching . . . but I've never seen a painting of Jesus spitting.

Christ smacking his lips a time or two, gathering a mouth of saliva, working up a blob of drool, and letting it go. Down in the dirt. Then he squats, stirs up a puddle of . . . I don't know, what would you call it?

Holy putty? Spit therapy? Whatever the name, he places a fingerful in his palm, and then, as calmly as a painter spackles a hole in the wall, Jesus streaks mud-miracle on the blind man's

The guy had to be thrilled. Or was he?

eyes. "Go, wash in the pool of Siloam" (John 9:7).

The beggar feels his way to the pool, splashes water on his mud-streaked face, and rubs away the clay. The result is the first chapter of Genesis, just for him. Light where there was darkness. Eyes focus, fuzzy figures become human beings, and John receives the Understatement of the Bible Award when he writes: "He . . . came back seeing" (John 9:7).

Come on, John! Running short of verbs? How about "He *raced* back seeing"? "He *danced* back seeing"? "He *roared* back whooping and hollering and kissing everything he could, for the first time, see"? The guy had to be thrilled. Or was he?

Emily was less than thrilled about her social studies class project on homelessness—especially the voluntary extra-credit part.

It wasn't that she wasn't sympathetic, or so she told herself that October morning in Miss Marsh's class. It was just that she had problems of her own to deal with right now. *Mom* problems. She simply didn't have time or energy for someone else's troubles. Besides, "those people" made her really . . . uncomfortable. Which, of course, made it all the easier to look away.

Unfortunately, looking away was *not* an option. And as for enthusiasm? Well, Miss Marsh had more than enough to go around. The pint-sized teacher was practically vibrating with conviction as she explained why they were going to love this "absolutely terrific opportunity to shake up your thinking."

Shake up our thinking?!

"You bet," said Miss Marsh. "Look, most of you have seen homeless people, and all of you have at least heard about the homeless 'problem.' Right?" Obedient nods all around.

"But," said Miss Marsh, "what do you really know about the what's, why's—and, most important, the

"What are you going to do about it?"

who's—of homelessness? What do you know about what it's like to *be* homeless?

"And then, of course," she added casually, "what are you going to do about it?"

Do about it?!

Miss Marsh nodded. "Trust me on this; you'll *want* to do something about it."

"But . . . but what can *we* do?" asked Josh.

"Oh, you'll think of something," came the cheerful answer. "But first things first . . ." There would be research, of course.

Lots of research: Print. Electronic. Interviews with homeless advocates. And, for those who wanted to volunteer for *extra* credit, supervised visits to homeless shelters, "to meet the people *inside* the problem."

Oh, great, thought Emily, *as if my life isn't depressing enough.* But the project was a done deal, like it or not. Emily definitely didn't like it. And Anna Crawford looked almost terrified for a fleeting moment. Of course, with Anna it was hard to tell. Who knew *what* the quiet newcomer who kept pretty much to herself really thought about anything? Certainly not Emily, who had other things on her mind. Like the mom situation. Or the slipping grades that might knock her off the honor roll.

Face it; I need all the extra credit I can get. So, when Miss Marsh asked who wanted a permission slip for the contact visits to homeless shelters, Emily sighed and raised her hand.

She was in. All the way. But she didn't have to be happy about it!

✣ ✣ ✣ We would love to leave the once-blind man in his moment of joy—but if this man's life were a cafeteria line, he would have just stepped from the sirloin to the boiled Brussels sprouts. Look at the reaction of the neighbors: "'Is not this the one who used to sit and beg?' Others were saying, 'This is he,' still others were saying, 'No, but he is like him.' He kept saying, 'I am the one'" (John 9:8–9).

These folks don't celebrate; they debate! They have watched this man grope and trip since he was a kid (John 9:20). You'd think they would rejoice. But they don't. They march him down to the church to have him priest-approved. When the Pharisees ask for an explanation, the was-blind beggar says, "He applied clay to my eyes, and I washed, and I see" (John 9:15).

Again we pause for the applause, but none comes. No recognition. No celebration. Apparently Jesus failed to consult the healing handbook. "Now it was a Sabbath on the day when Jesus made the clay and opened his eyes. . . . The Pharisees were saying, 'This man is not from God, because He does not keep the Sabbath'" (John 9:14, 16).

Huh?! In case you're confused, here's a parallel to the religious leaders' verdict. Suppose the swimming pool you visit has a sign that reads "Rescues Performed by Certified Lifeguards Only." You never think much about the rule until one day you bang your head on the bottom. You black out, ten feet under.

Next thing you know, you're belly-down on the side of the pool, coughing up water. Someone rescued you. And when the lifeguards appear, the fellow who pulled you out of the deep disappears. As you come to your senses, you tell the story. But rather than rejoice, people recoil. "Doesn't count! Doesn't count!" they shout. "It wasn't official. Wasn't legal. Since the rescuer wasn't certified, consider yourself drowned."

Duh? Will no one rejoice with this man? The neighbors didn't. The preachers didn't. Wait, here come the parents. But their reaction is even worse.

They called the parents of the very one who had received his sight, and questioned them, saying, "Is this your son, who you say was born blind? Then how does he now see?" His parents answered them and said, "We know that this is our son, and that he was born blind; but how he now sees, we do not know; or who opened his eyes, we do not know. Ask him; he is of age, he will speak for himself." His parents said this because they were afraid of the Jews; for the Jews had already agreed that if anyone confessed Him to be Christ, he was to be put out of the synagogue. (John 9:18–22)

How can they do this? Granted, to be put out of the synagogue is serious. But isn't refusing to help your child even more so?

Who was really blind that day? The neighbors didn't see the man; they saw a novelty. The church leaders didn't see the man; they saw a technicality. The parents didn't see their son; they saw a social difficulty. In the end, no one saw him. "So they put him out" (John 9:34).

Who was really blind that day?

"'The People No One Sees.' That's it!" Emily's excited voice cut through the silence. "That's the title for our CD," she explained to her startled classmates.

"Not bad . . . ," said Josh. "Not bad at all."

"Not bad?! It's perfect!" corrected Tracy.

Emily's proposed title even won one of Anna Crawford's rare smiles. Miss Marsh smiled, too. She was so proud of the way her class had dug into their homeless project. Best of all was the *distance* they'd traveled since last fall—a distance measured not in miles or months but in understanding and compassion. And then there was the CD: the one they were recording this afternoon in the Media Department—to speak, not about, but *for*, the homeless.

Of course, none of it had happened all at once, or easily. Not everyone had shared Miss Marsh's enthusiasm at the beginning. But—between the surprises revealed by their research and the unexpected people they met at the shelters— even the foot draggers were soon charging full speed ahead.

Emily Merrill had gone from grudging participation to reluctant interest to somebody-should-do-*something!* commitment. And even quiet little Anna Crawford would occasionally amaze everyone—including herself—by blurting out some surprising, and incredibly accurate, information she'd picked up "oh, . . . somewhere."

> **The average age of a homeless person in America is *nine years old!***

The entire class was determined to make some kind of difference, no matter how small. The things they'd learned had, indeed, shaken up their thinking. But it was the number of *families* at the shelters they'd found hardest to accept—along with the news from the National Coalition for the Homeless that the average age of a homeless person in America is *nine years old!*

"That can't be right!" Emily had protested. But it was. Correct, but not *right*. "We've got to do something," she insisted, "something to make the people inside the statistics *real* to everyone!" And so the idea for the CD was born. Everyone in class—even those with a bad case of mic-fright—would become the "voice" of someone they'd met or heard about at the shelters. It was brilliant. It was scary. It was perfect!

Josh kicked off the recording session. "My name is Marcus. I'm five years old, and I live at the homeless shelter. A lady gave me my first crayon today. It was red. But when she asked me to draw a house, I didn't know what a house looked like. . . ."

"My name is Mary," began Tracy. "I'm twenty-seven. When I lost my job last year and couldn't find another one, my kids and I ended up on the streets. . . ."

"You can call me Sam . . . and you can call me homeless. And if you think it's because I *want* to be, let me tell you about getting sick with no health insurance. . . ."

One by one, the names and stories unfolded. But it was what Anna Crawford had to say when her turn came that stunned everyone—including Miss Marsh.

"My name is Anna. I'm fourteen years old. And I don't have to *imagine* what it's like to be homeless. I *know*, because I am. . . ." [‡]

❋ ❋ ❋ Imagine how he felt—that man Jesus healed—abandoned by everyone because they saw a problem instead of a miracle. And now, here he is, back on the streets of Jerusalem. The fellow had to be bewildered. Born blind only to be healed. Healed only to be kicked out. Kicked out only to be left alone.

[‡] For more about Anna, see chapter 12.

The peak of Everest and the heat of the Sahara, all in one Sabbath. Now he can't even beg anymore. How would that feel?

You may know all too well. I know of a man who has buried four children. A single mother in our church is raising two autistic sons. We buried a neighbor whose cancer led to heart trouble, which created pneumonia. Do some people seem to be dealt more than their share of bad hands?

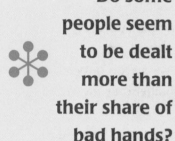

Do some people seem to be dealt more than their share of bad hands?

If so, Jesus knows. He knows how they feel, and he knows where they are. "Jesus heard that they had thrown him out, and went and found him" (John 9:35 MSG). In case the stable birth wasn't enough. If three decades of earth walking and miracle working are insufficient. If there be any doubt regarding God's full-bore devotion, he does things like this. He tracks down a troubled pauper.

The beggar lifts his eyes to look into the face of the One who started all this. Is he going to criticize Christ? Complain to Christ? You couldn't blame him for doing both. After all, he didn't volunteer for the disease or the deliverance. But he does neither. No, "he worshiped Him" (John 9:38). Don't you know he knelt? Don't you think he wept? And how could he keep from wrapping his arms around the waist of the One who gave him sight? He worshiped him.

And when you see him, you will, too.

How dare I make such a statement? This book will be held by crippled hands. These chapters will be read by tear-filled eyes. Some of your legs are wheelchaired, and your hearts are hope-starved. But "these hard times are small potatoes compared to the coming good times, the lavish celebration prepared for us" (2 Corinthians 4:17 MSG).

Emily smiled to herself amid the cheerful hum of the homeless-shelter dining room. Good. Everyone had plenty to eat, and they seemed to have left their troubles at the door. Then she positively beamed as she looked down into the solemn eyes of the small boy in line. *"There* you are, Marcus. I've been saving this just for you." She winked as she slid the pinkest, juiciest slice of ham onto his plate. "Happy Easter."

"Don't you just want to *hug* him?" Emily whispered to her mom as Marcus and his mother moved on down the serving line.

"Absolutely," agreed her mother, spooning a generous dollop of mashed potatoes onto the next plate. "And," she added with a grin, "he's not the *only* one."

"Moth-er!" But Emily was grinning, too. And she got *her* hug in first. *Really,* she thought, *life is good. Especially since Mom and I started getting along.*

Of course, that hadn't happened all at once, either—any more than Emily's change of mind, and heart, about homeless people. But, blessedly, it had happened.

She and her mom had always been close—until last summer, when things changed. Emily wanted to be independent, make her own choices—and mistakes. Her mom didn't like being shut out of Emily's life. Before either of them quite knew what had happened, Emily's biggest fan seemed to become her biggest critic—or at least that's how Emily saw things.

It was something Anna Crawford said one day at lunch that changed her point of view. "But that's what moms *do*, Emily. Fuss over us. Try to keep us from making mistakes. I don't know what I'd do without *my* mom!"

 "But that's what moms *do*, Emily. "

To tell the truth, Emily didn't know what she'd do without *her* mom—criticisms and all—either. *Maybe if I included her a little more . . .*

Emily was amazed at the way her mom jumped at the chance when she'd hesitantly asked, "I don't suppose you'd like to volunteer with me to serve Thanksgiving dinner at the homeless shelter?" Yes! came the answer. And they enjoyed it so much, they hadn't missed a holiday meal at the shelter since. Even though her school project was over, Emily's interest in helping the homeless wasn't. She still volunteered at the shelter—playing with the little kids, tutoring some of the older ones. And she was still thrilled about all the money her class CD had helped raise for local shelter programs.

And to think I almost missed it all because I was looking *instead of* seeing *the first time I came here.*

"How depressing!" she'd muttered to Stacy that first visit.

"Oh, my," said a silver-haired shelter worker who'd overheard. "That's because you're looking with your eyes instead of your heart."

"Well," Emily challenged, "what do *you* see when you look at these . . . these people?"

That got a grandmotherly smile, and a bolt-from-the-blue change of perspective for Emily. "My dear, I see Jesus."

❈ ❈ ❈ The day you see your Savior, you will experience a million times over what Joni Eareckson Tada experienced on her wedding day. Joni was just seventeen when a diving accident left her paralyzed. Nearly all of her fifty-plus years have been spent in a wheelchair. Her handicap doesn't keep her from writing or painting or speaking about her Savior. Nor did her handicap keep her from marrying Ken. But it almost kept her from the joy of the wedding.

She'd done her best. Her gown was draped over a thin wire mesh covering the wheels of her motorized wheelchair. With flowers in her lap and a sparkle in her eye, she felt "a little like a float in the Rose Parade."

While waiting to motor down the aisle, Joni made a discovery. Across her dress was a big, black grease mark, courtesy of the chair. And the chair, though "spiffed up . . . , was still the big, clunky thing it always was." Then the bouquet of daisies on her lap slid off-center; her paralyzed hands were unable to rearrange them. She felt far from a picture-perfect bride. Until . . . she looked down the aisle, and saw her groom.

I spotted him way down front, standing at attention and looking tall and elegant in his formal attire. My face grew hot. My heart began to pound. Our eyes met and, amazingly, from that point everything changed.

How I looked no longer mattered. I forgot all about my wheelchair. Grease stains? Flowers out of place? Who cares? No longer did I feel ugly or unworthy; the love in Ken's eyes washed it all away.[1]

When she saw him, she forgot about herself.

When you see him, you will, too.

I'm sorry about your greasy gown. And your flowers—they tend to slide, don't they? Who has an answer for the diseases, drudgeries, and darkness of this life? I don't. But we do know this. Everything changes when you look at your groom.

> When you see Jesus, you will bow in worship.

And yours is coming. Just as he came for the blind man, Jesus is coming for you. The hand that touched the blind man's shoulder will touch your cheeks. The face that changed his life will change yours.

And when you see Jesus, you will bow in worship.

CHAPTER 7

IT'S NOT UP TO YOU
(SPIRITUALLY CONFUSED PEOPLE)

JOHN 3:1-16

[Jesus said,] "Do not be amazed that I said to you, 'You must be born again.' The wind blows where it wishes and you hear the sound of it, but do not know where it comes from and where it is going; so is everyone who is born of the Spirit."
Nicodemus said to Him, "How can these things be?"

—John 3:7–9

✳ ✳ ✳ My dog Molly and I aren't getting along. The problem is not her personality. A sweeter mutt you will not find. She sees every person as a friend and every day as a holiday. I have no problem with Molly's attitude. I have a problem with her habits.

Eating scraps out of the trash. Licking dirty plates in the dishwasher. Dropping dead birds on our sidewalk and stealing bones from the neighbor's dog. Shameful! Molly rolls in the grass, does her business in the wrong places, and, I'm embarrassed to admit, quenches her thirst in the toilet.

Now what kind of behavior is that?

Dog behavior, you reply.

You are right. So right. Molly's problem is not a Molly problem. Molly has a dog problem. It is a dog's nature to do such things. And it is her nature that I wish to change. Not just her behavior, mind you. A canine obedience school can change what she does; I want to go deeper. I want to change who she is.

Here is my idea: a me-to-her transfusion. The deposit of a Max seed in Molly. I want to give her a kernel of human character. As it grew, would she not change? Her human nature would enlarge, and her dog nature would shrink. We would witness not just a change of habits, but a change of essence. In time, Molly would be less like Molly and more like me, sharing my disgust for trash snacking, potty slurping, and dish licking. She would have a new nature. Why, my wife, Denalyn, might even let her eat at the table.

God changes our nature from the inside out!

You think the plan is crazy? Then take it up with God. The idea is his.

What I would like to do with Molly, God does with us. He changes our nature from the inside out! "I will put a new way of thinking inside you. I will take out the stubborn hearts of stone from your bodies, and I will give you obedient hearts of flesh. I will put my Spirit inside you and help you live by my rules and carefully obey my laws" (Ezekiel 36:26–27 NCV).

God doesn't send us to obedience school to learn new habits; he sends us to the hospital to be given a new heart. Forget training; he gives transplants.

Sound bizarre? Imagine how it sounded to Nicodemus—a very godly, churchy man of Jesus' time who felt he was missing the boat spiritually.

It wasn't what Zoe was used to—this feeling of drifting aimlessly, with no control over where she was going, or what might happen next. And—much as she loved being with her aunt Kyra—she still had a few doubts about *this* particular adventure.

Zoe much preferred being in charge of every detail of her life. In fact—and she'd tell you this herself—she was something of a "control freak." Always had been. On toddler Zoe's dinner plate, the peas didn't dare touch the mashed potatoes—and the applesauce had better stay where it belonged, too! As she grew older, she always colored *inside* the lines; she never lost her homework; and if you played a game with her, you'd better know all the rules. Zoe certainly did.

By the time she reached eighth grade, Zoe could have been the poster girl for Organized Living. Her calendar was filled in through October. *Next* October. She knew the exact color of the dress she'd wear to her senior prom in four years. Teal blue. She'd already applied for three part-time jobs to be sure of having one year after next, when someone could actually hire her.

Zoe loves order and predictability and runs her life with

by-the-book precision. So why, then, does she feel so *disorganized* when it comes to her faith? She can quote Scripture with the best of them, and the youth-group projects she heads are flawlessly organized. So why doesn't she feel *connected* to God?

So why doesn't she feel *connected* to God?

She used to. But somehow, somewhere along the way, they seem to have lost touch. And the harder she worked at regaining that sense of closeness (and Zoe was a firm believer in planning and hard work to get the desired result) the farther away God seemed. And she had no more idea of what to try next than . . . than she could see what was beyond the next bend of the river she and Aunt Kyra were rafting.

"Who knows what's ahead, sweetie?" her aunt had answered, smiling at Zoe's attempts to peer *through* the rock of the canyon wall. "A surprise. A problem. A gift. A mystery. Whatever it is, it's God's hand at work. And that's good enough for me."

"But . . . ," began Zoe.

"But?" encouraged Aunt Kyra.

"Never mind," said Zoe. But what she wanted to say was, "But why can't I feel it?"

✳ ✳ ✳ It was never far from Nicodemus's mind—his feeling of separation from God. Finally, he couldn't stand it any longer, and he asked for help.

There was a man of the Pharisees, named Nicodemus, a ruler of the Jews; this man came to Jesus by night and said to Him, "Rabbi, we know that You have come from God as a teacher; for no one can do these signs that You do unless God is with him." (John 3:1–2)

Nicodemus is impressive. Not only is he one of the six thousand Pharisees, he is one of seventy men who serve on the high council. Think of him as a religious blue blood. What the justices are to the Supreme Court, he is to the Law of Moses. Expert. Credentials trail his name like a robe behind a king. When it comes to religion, he is loaded. When it comes to life, he's tired.

As a good Jew, he's trying to obey the religious rules. No small task. He has twenty-four chapters of laws regarding the Sabbath alone. Just a sampling:

- Don't eat anything larger than an olive. And if you bite an olive and find it to be rotten, what you spit out is still part of your allowance.

- You can carry enough ink to draw two letters, but baths aren't allowed for fear of splashing the floor and washing it.

- Tailors can carry no needles.

- Kids can toss no balls. No one can carry a load heavier than a fig, but anything half the weight of a fig can be carried twice.

Whew!

Can a scientist study stars and not be amazed at their splendor? Cut apart a rose and never notice its perfume? Can a theologian study the Law until he decodes the shoe size of Moses but still lack the peace needed for a good night's sleep?

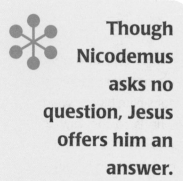

Though Nicodemus asks no question, Jesus offers him an answer.

Maybe that's why Nicodemus comes at night. He is tired but can't sleep. Tired of rules and regulations but no rest. Nicodemus is looking for a change. And he has a hunch Jesus can give it.

Though Nicodemus asks no question, Jesus offers him an answer. "Truly, truly, I say to you, unless one is born again he cannot see the kingdom of God" (John 3:3).

This is radical language. To see the kingdom of God, you need a rebirth from God. Nicodemus is astonished. "How can a man be born when he is old? He cannot enter a second time into his mother's womb and be born, can he?" (John 3:4).

Don't you love those last two words? *Can he?* Nicodemus knows that a grown man can't turn back into a baby. There is no rewind button on the VCR of life . . . is there? We don't get to start over . . . do we? A man can't be born again . . . can he? What makes Nicodemus add those two words? Old Nick should know better. He wasn't born yesterday.

But maybe he wishes he had been. Maybe those last two

words—"can he?"—come from that part of Nicodemus that longs for the strength of youth.

Nicodemus seems to be saying, "Jesus, I've got the spiritual energy of an old mule. How do you expect me to be born again when I can't even remember if figs can be eaten on the Sabbath? I'm an old man. How can a man be born when he is old?" According to Christ, the new birth must come from a new place. "The truth is, no one can enter the Kingdom of God without being born of water and the Spirit. Humans can reproduce only human life, but the Holy Spirit gives new life from heaven" (John 3:5–6 NLT).

Could Jesus be more direct? "*No one* can enter the Kingdom of God without being born of water and the Spirit." You want to go to heaven? Doesn't matter how religious you are or how many rules you keep. You need a new birth; you need to be "born of water and the Spirit."

God gives no sponge baths. He washes us from head to toe. Paul reflected on his conversion and wrote: "He gave us a good bath, and we came out of it new people, washed inside and out by the Holy Spirit" (Titus 3:5 MSG). Your sins stand no chance against the fire hydrant of God's grace.

First a splash . . . then a stream . . . then a shower of icy water drenched Zoe. Then, just as quickly, their raft moved beyond the ribbon of waterfall dropping from the canyon rim.

"See?" said equally soaked Aunt Kyra. "A gift. Feels good, doesn't it?"

Once she got over the shock, Zoe had to admit her unexpected shower *did* feel good in the heat of the August afternoon. In fact, everything about this rafting trip with her favorite aunt—contrary as it was to Zoe's usual structured approach to life—felt surprisingly . . . right. Although she *might* have preferred to skip one or two items on their non-agenda. Like that bit of frantic paddling through a suddenly-there stretch of rapids. Or the mysterious night noises that serenaded their shoreline campsites.

Zoe was not sorry, though, about saying "Yes!" when her free-spirited aunt had invited her along. "Just a few days rafting through Meridian Canyon, Zoe. See what turns up. Take a few photos. You know," she'd added with a teasing smile, "go with the flow.'" While Zoe might have preferred to organize and *direct* the flow, time with her aunt was too rare a treat to miss.

Kyra Martin was the beloved maverick in a family of solid citizens. *They* went to college. *She* joined the Peace Corps. *They* became doctors, lawyers, accountants. *She* was a nature photographer—a very talented one, already well known in her field.

The luminous, otherworldly quality of a Kyra Martin photo always won a second look. Every haunting image made you feel that something wonderful had just happened . . . or was *about* to happen.

When Zoe asked how she did it, Kyra just shrugged and laughed. "I wish I knew. I just find a subject I like, wait for the perfect moment, then hold my breath until . . ."

"Until?"

"Until I feel God in the picture. Then I snap the shutter. That's all."

That's all?! She makes it sound so . . . easy, thought Zoe, who'd tried everything she could think of to feel God in her own daily life.

It wasn't that Aunt Kyra was "religious," or broke out in prayer at inconvenient moments. In fact, she rarely mentioned God at all . . . she just sort of seemed to *assume* he was always there. Not at all like Zoe—who had put a lot of thought and effort into trying to get in touch with him this past year.

Zoe had read so much Scripture she was practically a Bible scholar! She'd thrown herself into church work. She lived her life the way she believed God wanted her to. But somehow, no matter how many times she dialed God's number, she couldn't even seem to get his voice mail!

> "**Maybe you're trying *too* hard.**"

"Maybe I'm not trying hard enough . . . ," Zoe said, staring dejectedly into the campfire.

"Or maybe . . . ," said Aunt Kyra, throwing in a hug, "maybe you're trying *too* hard—stretching too far for what's already there."

Already there?!

❅ ❅ ❅ When God washes you through the Holy Spirit, he's not content to simply clean you; he indwells you. God deposits within you "His power, which mightily works" (Colossians 1:29).

He does not do with you what my dad did with my brother and me. Our high-school car was a tired, messy old clunker.

Our lawn mower had more power. The car's highest speed, downhill with a tailwind, was fifty miles per hour. To this day, I'm convinced that my father searched for the slowest possible car and bought it for us.

When we complained about its pitiful shape, he just smiled and said, "Fix it up." We did the best we could. We cleaned the carpets, sprayed air freshener on the seats, painted the tires black. The car looked better, smelled better, but ran the same. Still a clunker—a clean clunker, to be sure—but still a clunker.

Don't for an instant think God does this with you. Washing the outside isn't enough for him. He places power on the inside. Better stated, he places *himself* on the inside. This is the part that stunned Nicodemus. Working for God was not new. But God working in him? *I need to think about that a bit.*

Maybe you do as well. Are you a Nicodemus? Feeling that no matter how much you do, it's not enough? If so, may I remind you of something?

When you believe in Christ, Christ works a miracle in you. "When you believed in Christ, he identified you as his own by giving you the Holy Spirit" (Ephesians 1:13 NLT). You are permanently purified and empowered by God himself. The message of Jesus to the religious person is simple: It's not what you do. It's what I do. I have moved in. And you are no longer a clunker, not even a clean clunker. You are now a sleek racing machine.

If that is true, Max, why do I still sputter? If I'm born again, why do I fall so often?

Why did you fall so often after your first birth? Did you

arrive wearing jogging shoes? Did you tap-dance on the day of your delivery? Of course not. And when you started to walk, you fell more than you stood. Should we expect anything different from our spiritual walk?

But I fall so often, I question my salvation. Again, we return to your first birth. Didn't you stumble as you were learning to walk? And when you stumbled, did you shake your head and think, *I have fallen again. I must not be human?*

If I'm born again, why do I fall so often?

Of course not. The stumbles of a toddler do not cancel his birth. And the stumbles of a Christian do not undo his spiritual birth.

"It was so easy when I was little," said a frustrated Zoe the next morning as they floated into the final miles of Meridian Canyon. "I felt God around me all the time."

"Sweetie," said Aunt Kyra, "*everything's* easier when we're little. But," she added cheerfully, "the older we get, the more *interesting* things get . . . if we pay attention."

Zoe wasn't exactly sure *what* that meant, but she did feel better for having shared her worries. Of course, she was still puzzling over what her aunt had said about "trying too hard" to connect with God. *But maybe it's worth a try*, she thought, then grinned, *to* not *try, that is.*

So for the rest of the day, Zoe stopped waiting for God to tap her on the shoulder and say, "Here I am, kid." Instead, she simply opened her eyes, like Aunt Kyra, to the silent ways he's always present: in tumbles of clouds decorating a sapphire sky . . . the dance of river light on canyon walls . . . the rainbow wing of a questing dragonfly. . . . There were moments—brief moments—when she got it. Then, as some plan or project would pop into her mind, she'd lose it again. But it was there. *He* was there. *There's got to be a way to hang on to this!*

"Aunt Kyra, how can I—" Zoe began as their raft floated into a quiet cove at the canyon's end. But her aunt was holding a silencing finger to smiling lips, and looking past Zoe into the cove where a family of wild swans floated on the sunlit water.

"Oh," breathed Zoe, "isn't it the sweetest thing!"

"And working so . . . *hard,*" whispered her aunt, as the baby of the family beat frantic wings in an effort to fly.

Flap-flap-flap. Flap-flap-flap. Nothing. Flap-flap-flap. Still nothing. The little guy sank back into the water. Then—maybe as a lesson, maybe just because she wanted to stretch her wings—its mother took to the air. With sure, graceful sweeps of snowy wings she lifted, circled upward, and rode the wind.

How beautiful! And how . . . easy. Zoe watched with shining eyes. The little swan watched as if it were taking notes. Zoe finally exhaled as the mother swan glided down to settle onto the water and give her baby an encouraging nudge. It gave it another try. Flap-flap-flap. Nothing. Flap-flap—just then, a puff of wind swept under the little swan's flurry of wings. And lifted it! But, instead of spreading its wings to let the wind carry it, it pumped even harder. Flap-flap-flap-FLAP. Then . . . PLOP, back into the water it dropped.

"Aw," said Zoe, "poor thing."

"Don't worry, sweetie," said her aunt, paddling them quietly out of the cove. "It'll catch on. After all, it was *born* to fly. All it has to do is learn to trust its wings . . . and the wind. And, of course," she added after a moment, "not—"

"—try quite so hard?" finished Zoe.

"Wel-l-l-l," came the answer, "maybe you *are* pumping just a tad too furiously to accomplish what God has *already* done for you."

> **God has already fixed you.**

Kyra smiled at Zoe's puzzled frown. "You're not broken, Miss Serious. God has already fixed you. And you don't have to look up or around or out to find him. He's a lot closer than that. Right here"—she placed a gentle finger over Zoe's heart—"inside you."

✳ ✳ ✳ Do you understand what God has done? He has deposited a Christ seed in you. As it grows, you will change. It's not that sin has no more presence in your life, but rather that sin has no more power over your life. Temptation will pester you, but temptation will not master you.

Nicodemuses of the world, hear this. It's not up to you! Within you abides a budding power. Trust him!

Think of it this way. Suppose for most of your life you have had a heart condition. Your frail pumper restricts your activities. When the healthy people take the stairs, you wait for the elevator.

But then comes the transplant. A healthy heart is placed within you. After recovery, you come to a flight of stairs. By habit, you start for the elevator. But then you remember. You aren't the same person. You have a new heart. Within you dwells a new power.

Do you live like the old person or the new? You have a choice to make.

You might say, "I can't climb stairs; I'm too weak." Does your choice cancel the presence of a new heart? No. Choosing the elevator would suggest only one fact—you haven't learned to trust your new power.

It takes time. But at some point you've got to try those stairs. You've got to test the new ticker. You've got to experiment with the new you. For if you don't, you will run out of steam. It's the same with your spiritual walk.

Religious rule keeping can wear you out. It's endless. There is always something else to "get right." No prison is as endless as the prison of perfection. Its inmates find work but never find peace. How could they? They never know when they are finished.

Christ, however, gifts you with a finished work. He fulfilled the law for you. Bid farewell to the burden of religion. Gone is the fear that having done everything, you might not have done enough. You climb the stairs, not by your strength, but his. God pledges to help those who stop trying to help themselves.

"He who began a good work in you will carry it on to completion until the day of Christ Jesus" (Philippians 1:6 NIV). God will do with you what I only dream of doing with Molly: change you from the inside out. When he is finished, he'll even let you sit at his table.

No Place He Won't Go

Charlie was ten. School was out for Christmas, and the family had chosen to spend the holiday in the country. The boy pressed his nose against the bay window of the vacation home and marveled at the British winter. He was happy to trade the blackened streets of London for the cotton-white freshness of snow-covered hills.

His mom invited him to go for a drive, and he quickly accepted. A wondrous moment was in the making. She snaked the car down the twisty road. The tires crunched the snow, and the boy puffed his breath on the window. He was thrilled. His mother, however, was anxious.

Heavy snow began to fall. Visibility lessened. As she took a curve, the car started to slide and didn't stop until it was in a ditch. She tried to drive out. The tires just spun. Little Charlie pushed, and his mom pressed the gas. But no luck. They were stuck. They needed help.

A mile down the road sat a house. Off they went and knocked on the door. "Of course," the woman told them. "Come in; warm yourselves. The phone is yours." She offered tea and cookies and urged them to stay until help arrived.

An ordinary event? Don't suggest that to the woman who opened the door. She has never forgotten that day. She's retold the story a thousand times. And who could blame her? It's not often that royalty appears on your porch.

For the two travelers stranded by the England winter were no less than Queen Elizabeth and the heir to the throne, ten-year-old Charles.[2]

The word on the streets of heaven and the lips of Christians is that something far grander has happened to our world. Royalty has walked down our streets. Heaven's prince has knocked on our door.

His visit, however, was no accident. And he did much more than stay for tea. Wood shops. Wildernesses. Under the water of the Jordan. On the water of Galilee. He kept popping up in the oddest places. Places where you'd never expect to spot God.

But then again, who would have expected to see him at all?

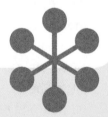

Heaven's prince has knocked on our door.

CHAPTER 8

HE LOVES TO BE WITH THE ONES HE LOVES (EVERYPLACE)

PHILIPPIANS 2:5-7

Have this attitude in yourselves which was also in Christ Jesus, who, although He existed in the form of God, did not regard equality with God a thing to be grasped, but emptied Himself, taking the form of a bond-servant, and being made in the likeness of men.

—Philippians 2:5–7

❊ ❊ ❊ Holiday time is travel time. Ever since Joseph and Mary packed their bags for Bethlehem, the birth of Jesus has caused people to hit the road. Interestingly, the Christmas trips we take have a lot in common with the maiden voyage of Jesus' folks. We don't see shepherds in the middle of the night, but we have been known to bump into an in-law on the way to the bathroom. We don't sleep in stables, but a living room full of sleeping-bagged cousins might smell like one. And we don't ride donkeys, but six hours in a minivan with four noisy kids might make some moms wish they had one.

"'Tis the season to be traveling." Nothing reveals the true character of family members like a long road trip.

> **Nothing reveals the true character of family members like a long road trip.**

We dads, for example, discover our real identities on the interstate. In the spirit of our *Mayflower* and Conestoga forefathers, we don't want to stop. Did Lewis and Clark ask for directions? Did the pioneers spend the night at a Holiday Inn? Did Joseph allow Mary to stroll through a souvenir shop in Bethlehem to buy an ornament for the tree?

By no means. We men have biblical permission to travel far and fast, stopping only for gasoline.

Wives, however, know the real reason we husbands love to drive: the civil war in the backseat.

Did you know scientists have proved that backseats have a wolfman effect on kids? Fangs, growls, claws. Social skills disappear into the same black hole as dropped French fries. Traveling siblings are simply incapable of normal human conversation. If one child says, "I like that song," you might expect the other to say, "That's nice." He won't. Instead, he will reply, "It stinks, and so do your shoes."

Then, of course, there are the teenagers. Teens are crawl-

under-the-car humiliated by their dads. They are embarrassed by what we say, think, wear, eat, and sing. So if dads seek peaceful passage, they'd better not smile in a restaurant, breathe, or sing with the window down or up.

Holiday travel. It isn't easy. Then why do we do it? You know the answer. We love to be with the ones we love.

The four-year-old running up the sidewalk into the arms of Grandpa.

Giggles and secrets with a favorite cousin long after everyone else is asleep.

That moment when, for a few seconds, everyone is quiet as we hold hands around the table and thank God for family and friends and pumpkin pie.

We love to be with the ones we love.

May I remind you? So does God. He loves to be with the ones he loves. How else do you explain what he did? Between him and us there was a distance—a great span. And he couldn't bear it. He couldn't stand it. So he did something about it.

Before coming to the earth, "Christ himself was like God in everything. . . . But he gave up his place with God and made himself nothing. He was born to be a man and became like a servant" (Philippians 2:6–7 NCV).

Jesus walked out heaven's door and hit the road. For us.

Jesus walked out heaven's door and hit the road. For us.

It wasn't your usual road trip. The mood swings inside the van filled with Edgemont Eagles made that clear. First, solemn silence. Then nervous chatter. Then silence again, soon interrupted by a cackle from Jose—who cracked up every time he looked at one of his teammates. *Any* one of them.

The thing was, they weren't at all sure *what* they should be feeling—up, down, or in between. So they felt it all. They were, after all, on pretty serious business. Yet the whole point of today's little excursion was to get—they hoped—a huge laugh. If all went well, that is.

Fortunately, the really *drastic* part of their plan was already done. They'd taken care of that right after the van had collected the last Eagle basketball player this morning. Now—still getting used to the results of Phase I—they were, for better or worse, on their way to execute Phase II of the plan. It had seemed like *such* a good idea when they came up with it. Of course, that was then . . . and this was now.

"What do you think Seth will say?" That from Corey, who was starting to wonder if they'd been as clever as they thought they were.

"Actually, I'm wondering what my *mom* will say," said Tim, meeting Jose's eyes in the rearview mirror.

"Man, you mean you didn't tell her?!"

"Nah," said Tim, "thought I'd save it for a surprise."

"Hope she *likes* surprises," said Jose doubtfully.

"Never mind Tim's mom!" interrupted Corey. "It's Seth I'm worried about. What if he . . . you know . . . takes it the wrong way?"

"Never happen," Steve assured him. "Seth's usually the guy who comes up with stuff like this."

"Yeah, but—"

"Besides," finished Steve, "we had to do *something*, didn't we?"

Everyone nodded. They were all in agreement about that. However Seth reacted, the important thing was that they'd be where they should be—they'd be with their friend.

❋ ❋ ❋ Why? Why did Jesus travel so far, put up with so much, for us?

I was asking myself that question when I spotted the squirrels outside my window. A family of black-tailed squirrels has made its home amid the roots of the tree north of my office. We've been neighbors for three years now. They watch me peck the keyboard. I watch them store their nuts and climb the trunk. We're mutually amused. I could watch them all day. Sometimes I do.

But I've never considered becoming one of them. The squirrel world holds no appeal to me. Who wants to sleep next to a hairy rodent with beady eyes? Give up the Rocky Mountains, bass fishing, weddings, and laughter for a hole in the ground and a diet of dirty nuts? Count me out.

But count Jesus in. What a world he left. Our classiest mansion would be a tree trunk to him. Earth's finest cuisine would be walnuts on heaven's table. And the idea of becoming a squirrel with claws and tiny teeth and a furry tail? It's nothing compared to God becoming a one-celled embryo, then a baby born in a stable.

But he did. The God of the universe was born into the poverty of a peasant and spent his first night in the feed trough of a cow. "The Word became flesh and lived among us" (John 1:14 NRSV). The God of the universe left the glory of heaven and moved into the neighborhood. Our neighborhood! Who could have imagined he would do such a thing.

Why? He loves to be with the ones he loves.

As the Edgemont Eagles rode through Seth's neighborhood they grew increasingly quiet. By the time their van pulled into his driveway, the silence was complete. How *would* Seth react to their "brilliant" plan? They no longer had any idea what to expect from their teammate, captain, and longtime friend.

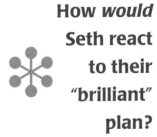

> **How *would* Seth react to their "brilliant" plan?**

On and off the basketball court, Seth had always been the spark plug that got things going—and the heart and soul of the fun and excitement that followed. He'd even taken the discovery of his leukemia last year in stride. "No big deal," he'd assured them. "The doctors know what they're doing, and there are all kinds of ways to beat this thing. I'll bounce back." And he had—even managing to play the final quarter of last spring's tournament game.

But that was then, this was now . . . and Seth's leukemia was back. This time, though, Seth—optimistic, fiercely determined, fast-with-a-wisecrack Seth—hadn't bounced back. Oh, he was out of the hospital, and the chemo treatments seemed to be working. But Seth? Well, that was another story.

Their up-for-anything buddy seemed to have lost his positive attitude and fighting spirit. In the past few weeks he'd hardly left his room at all. As for visits from friends, or even phone calls . . . forget it. Seth was discouraged, withdrawn, and in serious need of cheering up. And, ready or not, here came the Eagles to do just that! As soon as they gathered their courage, that is.

"Well," demanded Steve, flipping up the hood of his new team sweatshirt, "are we going to sit here all day?!" No they weren't! One by one they all flipped up their hoods, too, and streamed from the van. "Let's do it!"

But "doing it" ran into an immediate obstacle.

"Sorry, guys," said Seth's dad, after three trips up the stairs to his son's room. "Seth says he just isn't up to visitors yet. But please don't give up," he added sadly.

"No problem, Mister G," said Steve. "Look," he pleaded, "ask him to at least come to his window. We've got something to show him. Tell him . . . tell him if he doesn't, Jose here is going to stand right under that window and serenade him!"

That got a laugh from Seth's dad—who'd heard Jose's enthusiastic attempts at song more than once. "That should do it," he agreed, heading back up the stairs. And it did.

The boys didn't know whether Seth was curious . . . too tired to argue . . . or in dread of another off-key Jose "concert." It didn't matter, because it worked, as desperate plans fueled by love sometimes do.

❊ ❊ ❊ Dr. Maxwell Maltz tells a remarkable story of a love that would make any sacrifice. A man had been injured in a fire while attempting to save his parents from a burning house. He couldn't get to them. They perished. His face was burned and disfigured. He mistakenly interpreted his pain as God's punishment. The man wouldn't let anyone see him—not even his wife.

She went to Dr. Maltz, a plastic surgeon, for help. He told the woman not to worry. "I can restore his face."

The man wouldn't let anyone see him—not even his wife.

The wife was unimpressed. Her husband had repeatedly refused any help. She knew he would again.

Then why her visit? "I want you to change my face so I can be like him! If I can share in his pain, then maybe he'll let me back into his life."

Dr. Maltz was shocked. He denied her request but was so moved by this woman's love that he went to speak with her husband. Knocking on the man's bedroom door, he called loudly, "I'm a plastic surgeon, and I want you to know that I can restore your face."

No response.

"Please come out."

Again there was no answer.

Still speaking through the door, Dr. Maltz told the man of his wife's proposal. "She wants me to make her face like yours in the hope that you will let her back into your life. That's how much she loves you."

There was a brief moment of silence, and then, ever so slowly, the doorknob began to turn.[3]

The look on Seth's face as he leaned out his window and looked down at his teammates was priceless. Resplendent in their maroon-and-gold sweatshirts—every pointy hood in the up position—they looked for all the world like a perfectly matched set of extremely tall yard-art gnomes! *What on earth . . . ?!*

"Hey, guys," Seth called out, when he could finally talk, "what's . . . what's up?" And his lips twitched.

"These?" Steve grinned, touching his hood. "Just wanted you to get the full effect of our new team sweats. Before we unveil them to the rest of the world," he added.

"Along with our new name," chimed in Jose, blessedly *not* singing.

"New name?" *They changed the team name? Without even asking what I thought?!*

"Yeah," said Corey, "one that seems more fitting, what with you being captain and all. See what you think."

In perfect unison the boys turned around to reveal the embroidered team name on the back of each sweatshirt. The Edgemont Eagles were now the Edgemont *Bald* Eagles!

"We think it kind of goes with our new look," Steve explained with a grin. And, again in perfect unison, they pushed off their hoods—revealing a row of fresh-from-the-barber, smoothly shaven heads, each as hairless as Seth's own!

You could have heard a pin drop. No one had any idea

what Seth was thinking. And Seth didn't know whether to laugh, or cry, or throw up his hands. So he did none of those things. Instead, he went downstairs and out into the yard to be where he belonged—with his friends.

"Whose hair-raising—or should I say hair-*razing*—idea was this anyway?"

Seth was back.

❋ ❋ ❋ The way the woman in Dr. Maltz's story felt for her husband is the way God feels about us. But he did more than make the offer. He took on our face, our disfigurement. He became like us. Just look at the places he was willing to go: feed troughs, carpentry shops, badlands, and cemeteries. The places he went to reach us show how far he will go to touch us.

He loves to be with the ones he loves.

Chapter 9

A Cure for the Common Life
(Ordinary Places)

MARK 6:3

"Is not this the carpenter, the son of Mary, and brother of James and Joses and Judas and Simon? Are not His sisters here with us?" And they took offense at Him.

—Mark 6:3

You awoke today to a common day. No butler drew your bath. No maid laid out your clothes. Your eggs weren't Benedict, and your orange juice wasn't fresh-squeezed. But that's okay; there's nothing special about the day. It's not your birthday or Christmas; it's like every other day. A common day.

So you climbed into a common car—or caught a common bus—for a ride to school. You've heard about executives and sheiks who are helicoptered to their offices. As for you, a stretch limo might take you to a prom some day, but the rest of the time it'll probably be sedans and minivans. Common vehicles.

Common vehicles that take you to another common day at school. You take it seriously, but you would never call it extraordinary. You're not clearing your calendar for Jay Leno or making time to appear before Congress. You're just making sure you get your assignments in, your work done, and your obligations met before the closing bell.

And then, of course, there are the lines. You stand in a lot of those. Lines in the cafeteria. Lines for the bus. Lines at the movie ticket window. If you were the governor or had an Oscar on your mantel, you might bypass the crowds. But you aren't. You are common.

A face in the crowd can feel lost in the crowd.

You lead a common life. Punctuated by occasional parties, treats, rewards, and surprises—a few highlights—but mainly the day-to-day rhythm that you share with the majority of humanity.

And, as a result, you could use a few tips. You need to know how to succeed at being common. Commonhood has its perils, you know. A face in the crowd can feel lost in the crowd. You tend to think you are unproductive, wondering if you'll leave any lasting contribution. And you can feel unimportant. Do commoners rate in heaven? Does God love common people?

God answers these questions in a most uncommon fashion. If the word *common* describes you, take heart—you're in fine company. It also describes Christ.

Christ, common? Come on. Since when is walking on water "common"? Speaking to the dead "common"? Being raised from the dead "common"? Can we call the life of Christ common?

Nine-tenths of it we can. When you list the places Christ lived, draw a circle around the village named Nazareth—a one-camel town on the edge of boredom. For thirty of his thirty-three years, Jesus lived a common life. Aside from that one incident in the temple at the age of twelve, we have no record of what he said or did for the first thirty years he walked on this earth.

It would be easy to assume that Ben Smith was as ordinary as his name. Nothing about him was designed to attract attention. He was not too tall, not too short; not too loud, not too quiet. He'd never be movie-star handsome, but neither did his face frighten horses or small children.

Ben was just . . . Ben. No paparazzi lurked in the bushes to film him taking out the garbage. No adoring crowds gathered to watch him wash the family car. No darting spotlights followed his progress down the hallway at school.

To make his natural camouflage even more complete, Ben's a "middle kid"—the *second* of the three Smith children. He was born on the exact day he was expected. He grew and developed in perfect step with every baby-book schedule. And he did it all without the least bit of fuss or bother. It was almost as if God had decided that his mom needed a little peace and quiet between the daredevil antics of his big brother and the squeals and giggles of his little sister.

Because he's perfectly content to do his own thing, Ben sometimes gets overlooked in the noisy confusion of the busy

111

Smith household. And he's okay with that. He knows his family loves him. His parents are always there when he needs them. And his life is filled to the brim with all kinds of interests and projects that seem to pop up wherever he looks. Oh, every so often he might wonder what it would be like to be special in some way . . . or to *do* special things. But the thought never lasts long; his lively imagination and friendly curiosity keep him much too busy.

There's nothing Ben likes better than sinking his teeth into some knotty puzzle or problem. He's the first to notice when a helping hand is needed. And he's an expert fixer of broken things—all *kinds* of broken things. He just doesn't make a big deal out of any of it. As far as Ben's concerned, he's just an ordinary kid, doing ordinary things.

Of course, eighty-year-old Mrs. Dawson down the block might not agree. Neither would a bunch of smarter-than-they-thought-they-were kids at the community center . . . or a small tabby cat waiting for adoption named Suzanne. And they should know.

❉ ❉ ❉ Were it not for a statement in Mark's Gospel, we would not know anything about Jesus' early adult life. It's not much, but just enough thread to weave a thought or two for those who suffer from the common life. Here is the verse:

"Is not this the carpenter . . . ?" (Mark 6:3).

(Told you it wasn't much.) Jesus' neighbors spoke those words. Amazed at his latter-life popularity, they asked, "Is this the same guy who fixed my roof?"

Note what his neighbors did not say:

"Is not this the carpenter who owes me money?"

"Is not this the carpenter who swindled my father?"

"Is not this the carpenter who never finished my table?"

No, these words were never said. The lazy have a hard time hiding in a small town. Hucksters move from city to city to survive. Jesus didn't need to. Need a plow repaired? Christ could do it. In need of a new yoke? "My neighbor is a carpenter, and he will give you a fair price." The job may have been common, but his diligence was not. Jesus took his work seriously.

And the town may have been common, but his attention to it was not. The city of Nazareth sits on a summit. Certainly, no Nazarene boy could resist an occasional hike to the crest to look out over the valley beneath. Sitting six hundred feet above the level of the sea, the young Jesus could examine this world he had made. Mountain flowers in the spring. Cool sunsets. Pelicans winging their way along the streams of Kishon to the Sea of Galilee. Thyme-besprinkled turf at his feet. Fields and fig trees in the distance. Do you suppose moments here inspired these words later? "Observe how the lilies of the field grow" (Matthew 6:28), or "Look at the birds of the air" (Matthew 6:26). The words of Jesus the Rabbi were born in the thoughts of Jesus the boy.

The Maker of yokes later explained, "My yoke is easy" (Matthew 11:30). The one who brushed his share of sawdust from his eyes would say, "Why do you look at the speck that is

> **Jesus took his work seriously.**

in your brother's eye, but do not notice the log that is in your own eye?" (Matthew 7:3).

He saw how a seed on a busy path took no root (Luke 8:5) and how a mustard seed produced a great tree (Matthew 13:31–32). Jesus listened to his common life.

 **You'll be amazed at some of the very ordinary places you'll find God.**

Are you listening to yours? Rain pattering against the window. Silent snow in April. The giggle of a baby in a busy store. Seeing a sunrise while the world sleeps. Are these not personal epistles? Can't God speak through a Monday commute or a friend's smile? Take notes on your life. Pay attention. You'll be amazed at some of the very ordinary places you'll find God.

If there *were* a world-class, best-of-the-best annual championship for paying attention, Ben Smith would have retired the trophy by now. Where other people might glance, Ben looked. Where other people might look, Ben . . . *saw*. He'd always been that way—"one of life's observers," his mother had said years ago. And because he did pay such careful attention, he saw a lot that other people missed—*and* did something about it.

There was Mrs. Dawson, for instance—one of Ben's favorite lawn-mowing customers. All the neighbors knew who the eighty-year-old widow was, but few of them knew her well. Besides, she seemed fine. And they were . . . busy.

Why, she's lonely! Ben realized after the umpteenth lemonade "break" Mrs. Dawson had insisted he take from mowing her lawn. That's when he started dropping by on *non*-mowing days, too—sometimes for just a few minutes, other times for longer visits. With never a dull moment either way.

Ben was fascinated with Mrs. Dawson's stories about "the olden days." She was equally intrigued by his various projects. She always wanted to know what his math "students" at the community center were up to, and she never got tired of hearing about his volunteer work at the animal shelter. That surprised him at first—Mrs. Dawson's spotless house didn't seem the kind of place a dog or cat would be welcome. But a lot of them had been welcomed there over the years. "But when my sweet little Jenny passed away, I just didn't have the heart to . . . well, you know . . . ," she said wistfully.

Then her face brightened. "I know I have a picture of her in here somewhere." And—as often happened—out would come another big box crammed with a jumble of photographs. Which was fine with Ben—he enjoyed these looks into the past as much as Mrs. Dawson did. And that gave him an idea. *What if . . .*

"Here she is," said Mrs. Dawson, plucking out the photo of a graceful little tabby cat reaching up a gentle paw to pat her owner's cheek.

"You know," said Ben, admiring the little cat in the photo, "these pictures should be in an album or . . . something."

"I know, dear," sighed Mrs. Dawson, "but I just never got around to it. And now it seems like such a *big* job. . . ."

Ben nodded. "You're right. It is a big job . . . for just one person. But my mom and her friends are really into this memory book thing. And some of my math kids could help sort the photos, and—"

"Oh, my," protested Mrs. Dawson, "that's a lot of bother for a lot of people . . . to record such an ordinary life."

Ben shook his head. "Oh, no, Mrs. Dawson," he said, handing her another photo, "not an ordinary life at all." Together they admired the picture of a young Caroline Dawson—trim in her army nurse uniform—smiling forever at her hero-soldier husband. "Not ordinary at all," Ben repeated.

❋ ❋ ❋ The next time your life feels ordinary, take your cue from Christ. Pay attention to your work and your world. Jesus' obedience began in a small-town carpentry shop. His uncommon approach to his common life groomed him for his uncommon call. "When Jesus entered public life he was about thirty years old" (Luke 3:23 MSG). In order to enter public life, you have to leave private life. In order for Jesus to change the world, he had to say good-bye to *his* world.

He had to give Mary a kiss. Have a final meal in the kitchen, a final walk through the streets. Did he ascend one of the hills of Nazareth and think of the day he would ascend the hill near Jerusalem?

He knew what was going to happen. "God chose him for this purpose long before the world began" (1 Peter 1:20 NLT). Every ounce of suffering had been scripted—it just fell to Jesus to play the part.

Not that he had to. Nazareth was a cozy town. Why not build a carpentry business? Keep his identity a secret? Return

in the era of guillotines or electric chairs, and pass on the Cross. To be forced to die is one thing, but to willingly take up your own cross is something else. Something hard to understand—until you add in love.

Some of Ben's friends didn't understand how he could spend so much time at the animal shelter. "Isn't it, like, really depressing . . . ," Jill had asked, "all those hurt or abandoned cats and dogs?"

"I suppose it would be," Ben had answered, " . . . if we weren't working so hard to help them and find them homes." Ben, in fact, had found homes for dozens of them himself—thanks to his Internet BLOG, "Love to Go."

The BLOG was one of his coolest ideas ever.

The BLOG was one of his coolest ideas ever. And so simple. Each week he'd post a photo of one of his four-footed projects; add a paragraph singing its praises; then offer some lucky caller "a friend for life." The calls came in. The animals went out. Everyone was happy.

He hoped he could do as well for Suzanne. He'd fallen in love with the forlorn little tabby cat the first time he'd seen her huddled in the back of her cage. "What's . . . what's wrong with her?"

"She's grieving, Ben," the shelter director told him. "She's a one-person cat . . . and her person died. None of her elderly owner's children or grandchildren could take her, so she ended up here."

"But we can help her, right?"

"I . . . don't know, Ben. She won't eat. And she doesn't want anyone to touch her. We've all tried, but maybe you . . ."

Ben had spent hours sitting by Suzanne's cage . . . talking. He told her what a pretty cat she was. Admired the black-and-gray tabby markings of her coat. Asked how she got that notch in the tip of her left ear. Told her everything would be all right.

Curled into a tight little ball with her nose buried under her tail, Suzanne seemed to ignore him. But every so often Ben would see a whisker twitch, or an ear swivel in his direction, and on he'd talk. Little by little, it worked. First she nibbled, then she ate. *Probably just to shut me up*, he thought. Recently, she'd even accepted a gentle caress now and then. But only from Ben. She'd retreat to the back of her cage for anyone else.

"I don't know if we'll be able to find her a home, Ben," the shelter director warned gently. "Suzanne isn't a young cat. And, sweet as she is, she's just an ordinary little tabby—who seems to have given up on life. Who would want her?"

Ordinary . . . Suzanne? I don't think *so!* Ben thought. Besides, Ben already had the perfect person in mind. All he had to do was convince her.

Ben carefully set Suzanne's carrier down on Mrs. Dawson's porch, opened its door, and crossed his fingers. Taking her time—*lots* of time—Suzanne stepped daintily out of the cage. She nosed curiously around the wicker furniture; gave a planter of geraniums an approving sniff; then—at last—strolled over to sit politely at Mrs. Dawson's feet.

Brilliant emerald eyes held a wordless conversation with faded blue eyes. For a long moment no one breathed. Then, with a soft chirrup of greeting, Suzanne sprang lightly into a welcoming lap—and lifted one delicate paw to gently pat Mrs. Dawson's cheek.

"Oh," said Mrs. Dawson.

"Prrrp?" said Suzanne.

"Yes!" said Ben—who knew love at first sight when he saw it.

❈ ❈ ❈ The wonder of love is the *wonders* it works. Alan and Penny McIlroy can tell you. The fact that they have two adopted children is commendable but not uncommon. The fact that they have adopted special-needs children is significant but not unique. It's the seriousness of the health problems that sets this story apart.

Saleena is a cocaine baby. Her birth mother's overdose left Saleena unable to hear, see, speak, or move. Penny and Alan adopted her at seven weeks. The doctor gave her a year. She's lived for six.

> **The wonder of love is the *wonders* it works.**

As Penny introduced me to Saleena, she ruffled her hair and squeezed her cheeks, but Saleena didn't respond. She never does. Barring a miracle, she never will. Neither will her sister. "This is Destiny," Penny told me. In the next bed one-year-old Destiny lay, motionless and silent. Penny will never hear Destiny's voice. Alan will never know Saleena's kiss. They'll never hear their daughters sing in a choir, never see them walk across the stage. They'll bathe them, change them, adjust their feeding tubes, and rub their limp limbs, but, barring God's intervention, this mom and dad will never hear more than we heard that afternoon—gurgled breathing.[‡]

As I left that day, I wondered, *What kind of love is this?* What kind of love adopts disaster? What kind of love looks into the face of children, knowing full well the weight of their calamity, and says, "I'll take them"?

When you come up with a word for such a love, give it to Christ. For the day he left Nazareth is the day he declared his devotion to you and me. We were just as helpless, in a spiritually vegetative state from sin. But God, "immense in mercy and with an incredible love . . . embraced us. He took our sin-dead lives and made us alive in Christ. He did all this on his own, with no help from us!" (Ephesians 2:4–5 MSG).

Jesus left Nazareth in pursuit of the spiritual Saleenas and Destinys of the world and brought us to life.

Perhaps we aren't so common after all.

[‡]Destiny went to be with Jesus on December 3, 2002.

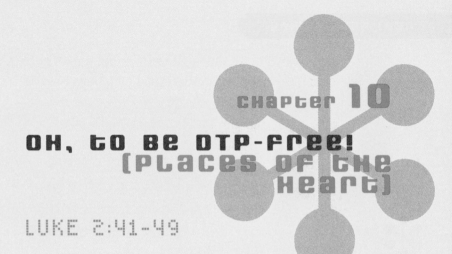

CHAPTER **10**

OH, TO BE DTP-FREE!
(PLACES OF THE HEART)

LUKE 2:41-49

When they saw Him, they were astonished; and His mother said to Him, "Son, why have You treated us this way? Behold, Your father and I have been anxiously looking for You."

And He said to them, "Why is it that you were looking for Me? Did you not know that I had to be in My Father's house?"

—Luke 2:48–49

❉ ❉ ❉ There was a time when only people and animals contracted viruses. A time when terms like *parasite* and *worm* were applied to living organisms and little brothers. A time when viral infections were treated by doctors and *quarantine* meant the isolation of diseased people and pets.

No longer. Nowadays, computers get sick. Preparation of this chapter would have begun several hours earlier had not a biohazardous, chemical-warfare-type warning put a freeze on my keyboard. "Open nothing! Your computer may have a virus!" I half expected Centers for Disease Control agents wearing radioactive gear to rush in, cover me, and run out with my laptop.

> **We call these DTPs: destructive thought patterns.**

They didn't, but a computer doctor did. He installed an antivirus program that protects the machine against 60,959 viruses.

I started to ask if Ebola was one, but I didn't. I did learn that hundreds of thousands of viruses have been created, I'm assuming by the same folks who spray graffiti on buildings and loosen salt shakers in restaurants. Troublemakers who Trojan-horse their way into your computer and gobble your data like a Pac-Man. I told the computer guy I'd never seen anything like it.

Later I realized I had. Indeed, a computer virus is a common cold compared to the Weapons of Mass Destruction-level attack you and I must face. Think of your mind as a computer made to store and process massive amounts of data (no comments about your neighbor's hard-drive capacity, please). Think of your strengths as software. Pianists are loaded with music programs. Accountants seem to be born with spreadsheet capacity. Fun lovers come with games installed. We are different, but we each have a computer and software, and, sadly, we have viruses. You and I are infected by destructive thoughts.

Computer viruses have names like Klez, Anna Kournikova,

and ILOVEYOU. Mental viruses are known as anxiety, bitterness, anger, guilt, shame, greed, and insecurity. They worm their way into your system and weaken, even disable, your mind. We call these DTPs: destructive thought patterns. (Actually, I'm the only one to call them DTPs.)

Do you have any DTPs?

When you see the successful, are you jealous?

When you see the struggler, are you smug?

If someone gets on your bad side, is that person as likely to get on your good side as I am to win the Tour-de-France?

Ever argue with someone in your mind? Rehash or rehearse your hurts? Do you assume the worst about people?

If so, you suffer from DTPs.

What if I miss? Don't even think *it, Lexie, failure is* not *an option!* A deep breath, a bound from the springboard, and Lexie flung herself into the air. Reaching . . . reaching . . .

It wasn't the first time that Lexie had had to throw herself into a new situation. It sometimes seemed that she'd been doing it all her life. So here she was—thanks to her dad's umpteenth job transfer—faced again with making a place for herself in a new school. And not just *any* old place, thank you very much!

The role of face-in-the-crowd was not for Lexie. She definitely wanted people to know she was there! Of course, that wasn't exactly easy to pull off—especially when you arrived late, weeks into the school year. But Lexie had a secret weapon few could match. It *always* got her noticed—though, to be honest, it hadn't exactly been a sure thing in the "making friends" department.

Slap! Chalked hands hit, and gripped, the high bar. Gathering momentum with a series of gliding swings, Lexie arced up and over into a picture-perfect handstand atop the bar. She held the difficult position for an impossibly long moment—then launched into a dazzling gymnastics routine on the uneven parallel bars.

With textbook precision, Lexie's slender body wove a graceful pattern of circles, spins, flips, and hold-your-breath release moves between the high and low bars. She capped her performance with a spectacular dismount—and, naturally, stuck her landing.

"Wow," said an awed Penny—finally remembering to breathe.

"My goodness," said Coach Andrews—wondering what this windfall of talent would mean for the Arlington Middle School gymnastics team.

"That," said Andrea, "was some . . . tryout." Then she grinned and added, "What else have you got?"

Uh-oh, thought Lexie, quick to hear a challenge—though Andrea's tone of voice didn't actually fall into that category. *Still . . .* "Oh, this and that," said Lexie, who had *everything* else, gymnastics-wise.

But instead of the jealous response Lexie expected: "Terrific!" said the dark-haired girl in the yellow leotard. "I'm Andrea; welcome to the team." And she seemed to mean it!

Which threw Lexie—sure-footed, always-in-control Lexie—

completely off balance. *Welcome? C'mon, you can't possibly be glad someone showed up to outshine you! Can you?* she thought.

Brilliant as she was at gymnastics, Lexie wasn't nearly as expert at figuring out people. Actually, she rarely tried. Most of her energy went into her athletic skills. She loved winning, and took pride in always being *best*. So she just assumed that everyone else felt that way, too.

What Lexie never quite caught on to was that seeing everyone as a possible *rival* kind of got in the way of finding many *friends*. So the girl who rarely missed on a vault, layout, or arabesque missed out on a lot of other things.

❊ ❊ ❊ What would your world be like without them [DTPs]? Had no dark or destructive thoughts ever entered your mind, how would you be different? Suppose you could relive your life without any guilt, vengeance, insecurity, or fear. Never wasting mental energy on gossip or scheming. Would you be different?

What would you have that you don't have? (Suggested answers found on page 133.)

What would you have done that you haven't done? (Suggested answers found on page 133.)

Oh, to be DTP-free. No energy lost, no time wasted. Wouldn't such a person be energetic and wise? A lifetime of healthy and holy thoughts would render anyone a joyful genius.

But where would you find such an individual? An un-infected computer can be bought—but an uninfected person? Impossible. Trace a computer virus back to a hacker. Trace our mental virus back to the fall of the first man, Adam. Because of sin, our minds are full of dark thoughts. "Although they knew God, they neither glorified him as God nor gave thanks to him, but their thinking became futile and their foolish hearts were darkened. Although they claimed to be wise, they became fools" (Romans 1:21–22 NIV).

Blame DTPs on sin. Sin messes with the mind. But what if the virus never entered? Suppose a person never opened Satan's e-mails? What would that person be like?

A lot like the twelve-year-old boy seated in the temple of Jerusalem. Though he was beardless and unadorned, this boy's thoughts were profound. Just ask the theologians with whom he conversed. Luke gives this account:

> [His parents] found Him in the temple, sitting in the midst of the teachers, both listening to them and asking them questions. And all who heard Him were amazed at His understanding and His answers. (Luke 2:46–47)

Jesus sought the place of godly thinking.

For three days Joseph and Mary were separated from Jesus. The temple was the last place they thought to search. But it was the first place Jesus went. He didn't go to a cousin's house or a buddy's playground. Jesus sought the place of godly thinking and, in doing so, inspires us to do the same. By the time Joseph and Mary located their son, he had astonished the most learned men in the temple. This boy did not think like a boy.

Why? What made Jesus different? The Bible is silent about his IQ. When it comes to the RAM size of his mental computer, we are told nothing. But when it comes to his purity of mind, we are given this astounding claim: Christ "knew no sin" (2 Corinthians 5:21). Peter says Jesus "did no sin, neither was guile found in his mouth" (1 Peter 2:22 KJV). John lived next to him for three years and concluded, "In Him there is no sin" (1 John 3:5).

Spotless was his soul, and striking was the witness of those who knew him. His fleshly brother James called Christ "the righteous man" (James 5:6). Pilate could find no fault in him (John 18:38). Judas confessed that he, in betraying Christ, betrayed innocent blood (Matthew 27:4). Even the demons declared his unique status: "I know who you are—the Holy One of God!" (Luke 4:34 NIV).

Lexie knew who would be her biggest competition on the Arlington gymnastics team from day one. It didn't take a rocket scientist to figure out that Andrea Kent was the team star. *But not for long,* Lexie promised herself—and went to work to claim that spot for herself.

The problem was, Andrea didn't seem to notice that they *were* in competition! Instead of resenting Lexie, Andrea seemed to actually enjoy the presence of a rival. Instead of being psyched out by some brilliant move, she'd ask Lexie to do it again—and would pay *very* close attention. And she was as generous with her compliments to Lexie as with the rest of the team. *What's going on here? Why is she being so . . . nice?*

Weeks into the team's best season ever, Lexie still couldn't figure it out. How could she and Andrea be so close in skills, when they were so far apart in every other way?

A rare mistake would devastate Lexie. Andrea would just laugh at her own goofs and get to work fixing them. Lexie had little patience with the shortcomings of others. Andrea was always the first with an encouraging word. Lexie was a perfectionist. Andrea was more of a—in her words—"perspectiv-ist." "Really, Lexie, it's not brain surgery or the formula for world peace. It's just a sport that's supposed to be, you know . . . fun?" she said once.

Lexie just shook her head and went back to work. But Andrea's laughing comment stuck with her. How could Andrea take something so important so . . . lightly? *Not take gymnastics seriously?! Why, without gymnastics I'd be . . . I'd be . . .*

Lexie's mental gears ground to a halt for a moment, then rolled relentlessly on. She'd never quite finished that thought before. That day she did, and it shocked her. *Without gymnastics I'd be . . . nothing. Wait, that can't be right!* But it seemed it was.

Ever since her outstanding talent had been recognized as a child, Lexie had made gymnastics the entire focus of her life. And why not? It was the one thing she did better than almost anyone else. It was the one thing she could always count on— *and take with her*—no matter where her dad's frequent job transfers sent them. Maybe she had gone a little overboard, but she had no earthly idea how to change direction now.

Besides, what's so wrong with working hard and making perfection your goal?! Unfortunately, what Lexie had forgotten—or never learned—is that there's perfection . . . and *perfection*.

✻ ✻ ✻ The loudest testimony of Jesus' perfection was the silence that followed this question. When his accusers called him a servant of Satan, Jesus demanded to see their evidence. "Which one of you convicts Me of sin?" he dared them (John 8:46). Ask my circle of friends to point out my sin, and watch the hands shoot up. When those who knew Jesus were asked this same question, no one spoke. Christ was followed by disciples, analyzed by crowds, criticized by family, and scrutinized by enemies, yet not one person would remember his committing even one sin. He was never found in the wrong place. Never said the wrong word. Never acted the wrong way. He never sinned. Not that he wasn't tempted, mind you. He was "tempted in all things as we are, yet without sin" (Hebrews 4:15).

He never sinned.

Anger wooed him. Greed lured him. Power called him. Jesus—the human—was tempted. But Jesus—the holy God—resisted. Contaminated e-mail came his way, but he resisted the urge to open it.

The word *sinless* has never fit any other person. Those who knew Christ best, however, spoke of his purity in unison and with conviction. And because he was sinless, his mind was stainless. DTP-less. No wonder people were "amazed at his teaching" (Mark 1:22 NCV). His mind was virus-free.

But does this matter? Does the perfection of Christ affect me? If he were a distant Creator, the answer would be no. But since he is a next door Savior, the reply is a supersized YES!

Remember the twelve-year-old boy in the temple? The one with sterling thoughts and a Teflon mind? Guess what. That is God's goal for you! You are made to be like Christ! God's priority is that you be "transformed by the renewing of your mind" (Romans 12:2 NIV). You may have been born virus-prone, but you don't have to live that way. There is hope for your head! Are you a worrywart? Don't have to be one forever. Guilt-plagued and shame-stained? Prone to anger? Jealousy? God can take care of that. God can change your mind.

Change isn't always comfortable. In fact, it can positively turn things inside out—as it did for Lexie. Not surprising, really; that's how change works . . . from the inside out.

Slap! Lexie's hands struck the high bar—and slipped off! *This can't be happening!* But it was—and, of all places, at the meet with archrival Northridge. It wasn't Lexie's first mistake. She'd been distracted all week by some pesky questions that just wouldn't go away:

Is looking for the worst in people *really* the way to see their best? When was the last time I threw out a compliment, instead of a criticism? Do I show people any reason to like me *other* than my gymnastics talent? And—this was the biggie—*is* winning the most important thing?

Andrea didn't seem to think so. "Well, sure, winning is fun," the dark-haired team captain had said. "But, hey, it's not the only thing that matters."

"Like . . . ?" asked Lexie, for whom it *was* the only thing.

"Oh, you know . . . ," Andrea had answered. "Friends. Being part of something bigger than yourself. The . . . *joy* . . . of the moment."

✻ ✻ ✻

Well, there's not much joy in this *moment,* thought Lexie, walking the endless miles back to the team bench. Her disastrous mistakes on the uneven bars—*and* the balance beam routine—would surely set a record for . . . incompetence!

"I'm . . . I'm sorry," she said, sitting next to Andrea. "I really let the team down." *The team?! Wait a minute . . . since when did I care more about the team than my own performance?* But, oddly, she did. It was very unsettling. "I don't know what's wrong with me."

"I do," Andrea assured her with a grin. "You're human, and we humans *do* have a tendency to goof every so often. Besides," she added, "who says you have to carry the *whole* load?"

That was typical Andrea, who seemed to be making a career out of catching Lexie off guard. *Okay,* thought Lexie, *as long as we're on the subject . . .* and she asked the question that had nagged at her from the very beginning. "This is going to sound strange, but . . ."

"I like strange," Andrea encouraged.

Lexie took a breath, then dived in. "Okay, I don't understand why it never seemed to bother you when I joined the team and . . . pushed . . . you so hard. Like you didn't mind not being . . ." Lexie swallowed the final word.

Andrea supplied it. "Best?" Then she laughed. "Lexie, it's never been about being *best.* It's about being the best *I* can be. And there's nothing like terrific competition to help me get there. Really, I should thank you." And she actually meant it.

Imagine that—a whole new way of thinking about competition or, for that matter, friendship: not what you get out of it, but what you put into it! Lexie wasn't sure she entirely got it, yet. But she was certainly going to pursue the thought.

✳ ✳ ✳ If ever there was a candidate for destructive thoughts, it was George. Abandoned by his father, orphaned by his mother, the little boy was shuffled from foster parent to homelessness and back several times. A sitting duck for bitterness and anger, George could have spent his life getting even. But he didn't. He didn't because Mariah Watkins taught him to think good thoughts.

The needs of each attracted the other—Mariah discovered the young boy sleeping in her barn, and she took him in. Not only that, she took care of him, took him to church, and helped him find his way to God. When George left Mariah's home, among his few possessions was a Bible she'd given him. By the time he left her home, she had left her mark on his soul.[4]

And by the time George left this world, he had left his.

George—George Washington Carver—is a father of modern agriculture. History credits him with more than three hundred products extracted from peanuts alone. The once-orphaned houseguest of Mariah Watkins became the friend of Henry Ford, Mahatma Gandhi, and three American presidents. He entered his laboratory every morning with the prayer "Open thou mine eyes, that I may behold wondrous things out of thy law" (Psalm 119:18 KJV).

God answers such prayers. He changes the man by changing the mind. And how does it happen? By doing what you are doing right now: considering the glory of Christ. "But we all, with unveiled face, beholding as in a mirror the glory of the Lord, are being transformed into the same image from glory to glory, just as from the Lord, the Spirit" (2 Corinthians 3:18).

To behold him is to become like him. As Christ dominates your thoughts, he changes you from one degree of glory to another until—hang on!—you are ready to live with him.

Heaven is the land of sinless minds. Virus-free thinking. Absolute trust. No fear or anger. Shame and second-guessing are practices of a prior life. Heaven will be wonderful, not because the streets are gold, but because our thoughts will be pure.

So what are you waiting for? Apply God's antivirus. "Set your mind on the things above, not on the things that are on earth" (Colossians 3:2). Give him your best thoughts, and see if he doesn't change your mind.

Answers to questions on page 125:
o More sleep, joy, and peace
o Hugged friends more, loved parents better, invented computer-virus killer, and traveled to Paris to watch Max win the Tour-de-France

*Jesus arrived from Galilee at the Jordan coming to John, to
be baptized by him.*

—Matthew 3:13

❊ ❊ ❊ No one pays him special attention. Not that they
should. Nothing in his appearance separates him from the
crowd. Like the rest, he is standing in line, waiting his turn. The
coolness of the mud feels nice between his toes, and the occasional lap of water is welcome on his feet. He, like the others,
can hear the voice of the preacher in the distance.

Between baptisms, John the Baptist is prone to preach.
Fiery. Ferocious. Fearless. Bronzed face, unshorn locks. His eyes
are as wild as the countryside from which he came. His whole
presence is a sermon—"a voice of one calling in the desert,
'Prepare the way for the Lord'" (Luke 3:4 NIV).

He stands waist-deep in the blue waters of the Jordan. He makes a wardrobe out of camel's hair, a meal out of bugs, and, most important, he makes a point of calling all people to the water. "He went into all the country around the Jordan, preaching a baptism of repentance for the forgiveness of sins" (Luke 3:3 NIV).

Baptism wasn't a new practice. It was required for any Gentile seeking to become a Jew. Baptism was for the moldy, second-class, unchosen people, not the clean, top-of-the-line class favorites—the Jews. And that raised some eyebrows, because John refused to differentiate between Jew and Gentile. In his book, every heart needed a detail job.

Every heart, that is, except one. That's why John is stunned when that One wades into the river.

> But John didn't want to baptize him. "I am the one who needs to be baptized by you," he said, "so why are you coming to me?"
>
> But Jesus said, "It must be done, because we must do everything that is right." So then John baptized him.
>
> After his baptism, as Jesus came up out of the water, the heavens were opened and he saw the Spirit of God descending like a dove and settling on him. And a voice from heaven said, "This is my beloved Son, and I am fully pleased with him." (Matthew 3:14–17 NLT)

A lot of parents might not know quite what to do with a son like Nick. Fortunately, his did. They simply . . . *appreciated* . . . him. Of course, his somewhat structured approach to life *did* take a little getting used to. Nick always liked—no, Nick always *had*—to know what would happen next. Even more, he wanted to know what he had to do to make *sure* it would happen the way he expected.

Nick was a planner, and not just an ordinary one, either. Most people might be satisfied with a Plan A, and *sometimes* a just-in-case Plan B. Not Nick. His strategies reached a lot farther than that into the alphabet—on one memorable occasion, all the way to Plan Z! Nick liked to be prepared—with a solution for any possible complication already figured out.

In fact, Nick liked planning so much that he often planned his way into some very elaborate—and some might say overly ambitious—projects. But, in spite of a few hair-raising moments here and there, he always managed to follow through on his promises. So—although they might sometimes shake their heads or throw up their hands—his family was really very proud of his enthusiasm and generous spirit. After all, he'd never actually bitten off more than he could chew. Until now, maybe.

His mom and dad didn't know whether to be impressed or alarmed when Nick casually mentioned his latest project. Yes, spiffing up the shabby Head Start center *was* a very worthy cause. And, yes, it *was* wonderful that so many plumbers and builders and electricians had donated their services. Too bad, though, about the problem finding painters. What? *Nick* had volunteered to see to it that the main classroom got a fresh coat of Primrose Yellow?!

"But isn't that sort of a . . . major . . . undertaking, son?

Promising to have that big room all painted by . . . when? . . . a week from Monday?!"

"No problem," said Nick, whipping out his ever-present clipboard. "Everything's arranged." And, indeed, it was. The hardware store owner had already agreed to donate all the Primrose Yellow they could use. Brushes, rollers, ladders, and tarps had been borrowed from an assortment of friends and neighbors. Nick had even talked some of the moms into scrubbing down the dirty walls as soon as they were patched. All that was left was brushing on the paint.

Even the most carefully structured plans can sometimes go awry.

"And I've got a bunch of friends lined up to help me with that next weekend." And he flipped to *that* neatly checked-off list. "See? No problem." And, indeed, there shouldn't have been. Of course, even the most carefully structured plans can sometimes go awry. Especially when something—or someone—totally unexpected turns up.

❋ ❋ ❋ John's surprise and reluctance to baptize Jesus is understandable. A baptismal ceremony is an odd place to find the Son of God. He should be the baptizer, not the baptizee. Why would Christ want to be baptized? If baptism was, and is, for the confessed sinner, how do we explain the immersion of history's only sinless Soul?

You'll find the answer in the pronouns: "Jesus answered,

'For now this is how it should be, because *we* must do all that God wants *us* to do'" (Matthew 3:15 CEV, emphasis mine).

Who is "we"? Jesus and us. Why does Jesus include himself? It's easy to understand why you and I and John the Baptist and the crowds at the creek have to do what God says. But Jesus? Why would he need to be baptized?

Here's why: Jesus did for us what I did for one of my daughters in the airport gift shop in New York. The sign above the ceramic pieces read "Do Not Touch." But the wanting was stronger than the warning, and she touched. And it fell. By the time I looked up, ten-year-old Sara was holding the two pieces of a New York City skyline. Next to her was an unhappy store manager. Over them both was the written rule. Between them hung a nervous silence. My daughter had no money. He had no mercy. So I did what dads do. I stepped in. "How much do *we* owe you?" I asked.

> **We've broken commandments, promises, and, worst of all, we've broken God's heart.**

How was it that I owed anything? Simple. She was my daughter. And since she could not pay, I did.

Since you and I cannot pay, Christ did. We've broken so much more than souvenirs. We've broken commandments, promises, and, worst of all, we've broken God's heart.

But Christ sees our plight. With the law on the wall and shattered commandments on the floor, he steps near (like a neighbor) and offers a gift (like a Savior).

Nick was in quite a predicament. His projects usually ran like clockwork. And, if things had gone according to plan, painting the Head Start center classroom would have been no exception—if it hadn't been for . . . the *complication*.

Her name was Belle Harris—"That's *Ms.* Harris"—and early this week she had tossed one very big monkey-wrench into Nick's smoothly running machine. She was small—though she somehow managed to take up the space of someone twice her size. She was impatient—"Don't have time to mess around, guys. Got a schedule to keep." And she had a clipboard even bigger than Nick's.

Ms. Harris was the building inspector who had to sign off on the improvements made to the center before it could open next Monday. And she had shown up, right on schedule, Tuesday afternoon to do just that. Unfortunately, there were a few minor plumbing and electrical glitches that didn't pass her eagle-eyed inspection. "Nope. Won't do. Can't approve occupancy till these are fixed . . . and fixed *right.*"

"No problem," said both electrician and plumber. "We'll have them ready for reinspection tomorrow afternoon."

Ms. Harris gave them a *look*. "No problem for you, maybe. *Big* problem for me. Got a busy schedule. Don't see how I can get back here for, oh, a couple of weeks."

"But," protested Nick, who'd come by with some more brushes and rollers, "it's supposed to open on Monday!"

"'Fraid it won't," said Ms. Harris, shaking her head. "Kind of a shame, too. But I'm booked solid."

"Well," suggested Nick, in full problem-solving mode, "how about Saturday? We'll be here finishing up the paint—"

"Saturday? Sonny, I work Monday through Friday. Nothing about any Saturdays in my job description. Got a life, you know."

And that, it seemed, was that. To everyone but Nick—who was nearly as stubborn as he was structured. He'd finish his part, no matter what! And . . . *and pray for a miracle, I guess.*

* * *

By Saturday afternoon, forget miracles, Nick would have settled for just a few *helpers!* No one—not a single one of the volunteer painters on his carefully detailed list—had shown up. Seems all his buddies—even his fallback crew—had found other things to do. "What's the rush *now*, Nick? The center can't open next week anyway, not without that final inspection."

Now with one enormous wall still to paint all by himself in the way-too-quiet building, Nick could see their point. But it was their point of view he had problems with. *Besides, a promise is a promise!* So he dipped his brush and got back to work—and nearly jumped out of his skin when the door banged open, and in walked . . . the complication.

"Wh . . . what are *you* doing here?"

"Wh . . . what are *you* doing here? I thought you didn't work on Saturdays?"

"Well," said Ms. Harris, as she checked out the plumbing and electrical repairs, "I guess that depends on what you mean by 'work.' Besides, you've got something pretty good going on here. So I guess maybe you *could* say I was wrong about not 'working' this weekend. Nobody's perfect, you know."

❋ ❋ ❋ We owe God a perfect life. Perfect obedience to every command. Not just the command of baptism, but the commands of humility, honesty, integrity. We can't deliver. Might as well charge us for all of New York City. But Christ can and he did. His plunge into the Jordan is a picture of his plunge into our sin. His baptism announced, "Let me pay."

Your baptism responds, "You bet I will." He publicly offers. We publicly accept. We "became part of Christ when we were baptized" (Romans 6:3 NCV). In baptism we identify with Christ. We go from shopper to buyer. We step out of the shadows, point in his direction, and announce, "I'm with him."

I used to do this at the drive-in movie theater. (Way before your time—ask your parents.)

The one in Andrews, Texas, had a Friday-night special—a carload for the price of the driver. Whether the car carried one passenger or a dozen, the price was the same. We often chose the dozen option. The law would not allow us to do today what we did then. Shoulders squished. Little guy on the big guy's lap. The ride was miserable, but the price was right. When the person at the ticket window looked in, we pointed to the driver and said, "We're with him."

God doesn't tell you to climb into Christ's car; he tells you to climb into Christ! "There is now no condemnation for those who are in Christ Jesus" (Romans 8:1 NIV). He is your vehicle!

Baptism celebrates your decision to take a seat. "For all of you who were baptized *into* Christ have clothed yourselves with Christ" (Galatians 3:27, emphasis mine). We are not saved by the act, but the act demonstrates the *way* we are saved. We are given credit for a perfect life we did not lead—indeed, a life we never could lead.

Give Nick credit: Surprised though he was by the building inspector's unexpected appearance, he *did* remember his manners.

"Wow, this is really nice of you, Ms. Harris. Coming in on a Saturday and all. Did . . . did the plumbing and electrical repairs pass inspection?" He held his breath, then let it all out in a *whoosh* of relief when she nodded. "Great! Now the Head Start center can open on time after all."

"Not so fast there, Flash." Her next words drenched his enthusiasm like a bucket of ice water. "I'm seeing an unfinished wall here. Not at all up to *my* standards."

Nick didn't know what to say to that. Even worse, he *did* know he couldn't expect her to wait around while he finished several hours of painting.

"Well . . . ?" said Ms. Harris, tapping an impatient foot.

Well . . . what?!

"Careful planner like you is bound to have at least *one* spare brush." He quickly found a brush and handed it to her.

Nick was speechless. But that was okay; Ms. Harris didn't want any thanks. "No problem," she said, brush flying, when he finally fumbled out a few words. "Consider it a gift."

✳ ✳ ✳ Through Jesus we are given a gift similar to the one pop musician Billy Joel gave his daughter. On her twelfth birthday she was in New York City, and Billy Joel was in Los Angeles. He phoned her that morning, apologizing for his absence, but told her to expect the delivery of a large package before the end of the day. The daughter answered the door that evening to find a seven-foot-tall, brightly wrapped box. She tore it open, and out stepped her father, fresh off the plane from the West Coast.‡

Can you imagine her surprise?

Perhaps you can. Your gift came in the flesh, too.

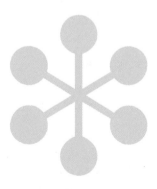

---

‡My thanks to Bob Russell for sharing this story.

Chapter 12

The Long, Lonely Winter [Wilderness Places]

LUKE 4:1-13

He led Him to Jerusalem and had Him stand on the pinnacle of the temple, and said to Him, "If You are the Son of God, throw Yourself down from here; for it is written, 'HE WILL COMMAND HIS ANGELS CONCERNING YOU TO GUARD YOU,' and 'ON their *HANDS THEY WILL BEAR YOU UP, SO THAT YOU WILL NOT STRIKE YOUR FOOT AGAINST A STONE.'"*

And Jesus answered and said to him, "It is said, 'YOU SHALL NOT PUT THE LORD YOUR GOD TO THE TEST.'"

When the devil had finished every temptation, he left Him until an opportune time.

—Luke 4:9–13

✻ ✻ ✻ The wilderness of the desert. Parched ground. Sharp rocks. Shifting sand. Burning sun. Thorns that cut. Wavy horizons ever beyond reach. This is the wilderness of the desert.

The wilderness of the soul. Parched promises. Sharp words. Shifting commitments. Burning anger. Rejections that cut. Distant solutions ever beyond reach. This is the wilderness of the soul.

Some of you know the first. All of you know the second. Jesus, however, knew both.

With skin still moist with Jordan baptismal water, he turned away from food and friends and entered the country of hyenas, lizards, and vultures. He was "led around by the Spirit in the wilderness for forty days, being tempted by the devil. And He ate nothing during those days, and when they had ended, He became hungry" (Luke 4:1–2).

The wilderness was not a typical time for Jesus. Normal life was left at the Jordan and would be found again in Galilee. The wilderness was and is outside the ordinary. A dark chapter in the story of life. A fierce season of face-to-face encounters with the devil.

You needn't journey to Israel to experience the wilderness. A cemetery will do just fine. So will a hospital. Grief can lead you into the desert. So can a parents' divorce or broken promises or a lost friendship.

I received word this morning of a friend who, thinking he was cancer-free, is going back for chemotherapy. Wilderness. I ran into a fellow at lunch who once talked to me about his tough marriage. I asked him how it was going. He shrugged. "It's going." Wilderness. Opened an e-mail from an acquaintance who is spending her summer at the house of her dying mother. Waiting. In the wilderness.

You can often chalk up wilderness wanderings to major change. Jesus entered the Jordan River a carpenter and exited a Messiah. His baptism flipped a switch.

Been through any big changes lately? A new school? Problems at home? Problems with friends? New responsibili-

Been through any big changes lately?

ties? If so, be wary. The wilderness might be near.

How do you know when you're in one?

You are lonely. Whether in fact or in feeling, no one can help, understand, or rescue you.

And your struggle seems endless. In the Bible, the number forty is associated with lengthy battles. Noah faced rain for forty days. Moses faced the desert for forty years. Jesus faced temptation for forty nights. Please note, he didn't face temptation for one day out of forty. Jesus was "in the wilderness for forty days, being tempted by the devil" (Luke 4:1–2). Jesus spent a month and ten days slugging it out with Satan. The wilderness is a long, lonely winter.

Problem after problem. Disappointment after disappointment. Failure after failure. Heartache after heartache. The calendar is stuck in February, and you can't even remember what spring smells like.

*   *   *

Like a dreary February day, there are a lot of things about being homeless that can get you—and keep you—down. Anna Crawford[‡] knows them all:

[‡]For more about Anna, see chapter 6.

- Wearing donated clothes—and dreading that some classmate might recognize a sweater or jacket that was once *hers*.

- Eating and sleeping in shelters—knowing that every bite and every night is charity.

- Having nothing, and no place, to call your own—and yearning for just a tiny bit of privacy.

- Seeing the way people look, or *don't* look, at you—until you start wondering if maybe you're not worth noticing after all.

Anna and her mom had lived hand-to-mouth for as long as Anna could remember. It wasn't that her mother didn't try for something better, but that's not so easy especially when minimum-wage jobs are all you can qualify for. Still, Mary Crawford never lost heart or hope. Somehow, with God's help, they always managed to make it through another month. Until . . .

Until Anna's mom got too sick to work.

Until the rent on their grim little apartment went from "a little late" to "very late" to "Evicted!"

Until they ended up on the street last year—and Anna got a crash course in being one of the "invisible" people.

But somehow, through it all, Anna never lost her absolute certainty about exactly who—and *what*—she was. And that made all the difference.

When she transferred to Ainsley High School—her third school in as many years—Anna was an old hand at fitting in without standing out. She was pleasant, but not outgoing, and in general did her best to just kind of blend into the background. And for the most part she succeeded.

Still, there was *something* about Anna that made people wonder. Her clothes might be secondhand, but no one walked the halls with a higher head, a straighter back, or more confident eyes. "Like she thinks she's some kind of . . . royalty," one girl had decided, half-critical, half-impressed. But since Anna did nothing else to make herself stand out, curiosity soon died. Which was fine with her. Yes, she'd *like* to have friends, but friends got to know a *lot* about each other.

> **Miss Marsh had no idea Anna was homeless.**

Anna wasn't ashamed of being homeless, but she sure didn't like what happened when people found out she was. Once people knew *that* about you, it suddenly became the only thing about you that mattered. So Anna took care that there was no opportunity for the issue of homelessness to come up. Unfortunately, Miss Marsh—who had no idea Anna was homeless—thought it was the *perfect* project for her social studies class!

Oh, no! was Anna's first thought, *what if they find out . . . ?* Then she remembered that school records were confidential. She'd just have to be careful, that was all.

Oh, well, was her next thought, *at least I'm way ahead of everyone else on the "research" part of the project!* She'd have to be careful about letting it show, of course.

But it would be okay. After all, Anna was something of an expert at facing up to tough challenges. In fact—considering who she was—doing anything else was, well . . . unthinkable!

❋ ❋ ❋ As if the loneliness isn't enough, here's one more symptom of the wilderness: You think the unthinkable. Jesus did. Wild possibilities crossed his mind. Teaming up with Satan? Opting to be a dictator and not a Savior? Torching Earth and starting over on Pluto? We don't know what he thought. We just know this: He was tempted. And "one is tempted when he is carried away and enticed by his own lust" (James 1:14). Temptation "carries" you and "entices" you. What was unimaginable prior to the wilderness becomes possible in it. A tough family situation can make leaving look good. Extended sickness makes even the stoutest soul consider giving up. Troubled relationships make angry words easier and quicker.

The wilderness weakens resolve and makes things you wouldn't ordinarily do seem like possible solutions. In the wilderness you think the unthinkable.

Jesus did. Jesus was "tempted by the devil" (Luke 4:2). Satan's words, if for but a moment, gave him pause. He may not have eaten the bread, but he stopped long enough in front of the bakery to smell it. Christ knows the wilderness. More than you might imagine. After all, going there was his idea.

Don't blame this episode on Satan. He didn't come to the desert looking for Jesus. Jesus went to the badlands looking for him. "The Spirit led Jesus into the desert *to be tempted* by the devil" (Matthew 4:1 NCV, emphasis mine). Heaven arranged this date. How do we explain this? The list of surprising places grows again. If Jesus in the manger and the Jordan waters doesn't stun you, Jesus in the wilderness will. Why did Jesus go to the desert?

Does the word *rematch* mean anything to you? For the second time in history, an unfallen mind will be challenged by the fallen angel. The Second Adam has come to succeed where the first Adam failed. Jesus, however, faces a test far more difficult. Adam was tested in a garden; Christ in a stark wasteland. Adam faced Satan on a full stomach; Christ is in the midst of a fast. Adam had a companion: Eve. Christ has no one. Adam was challenged to remain sinless in a sinless world. Christ, on the other hand, is challenged to remain sinless in a sin-filled world.

Stripped of any aid or excuses, Christ dares the devil to climb into the ring. "You've been haunting my children since the beginning. See what you can do with me." And Satan does. For forty days the two go toe-to-toe. The Son of heaven is tempted but never wavers, struck but never struck down. He succeeds where Adam failed. This victory, according to Paul, is a huge victory for us all. "Here it is in a nutshell: Just as one person did it wrong and got us in all this trouble with sin and death, another person did it right and got us out of it" (Romans 5:18 MSG).

There was no one to get her out of it—and no way to avoid it—so Anna was stuck. Like it or not, there was going to be a class project on homelessness.

"Oh, my," said her mother, trying to be serious but unable

to hide a smile when she heard the news. "Do you suppose God might be playing around here . . . just a little?"

"Probably," said Anna, who'd been wondering exactly that. "After all, what would be the point of inventing humor if he never got to use it himself?"

Neither of them found anything at all strange about their late-night conversation in the shelter dormitory. God was so much a part of their lives that they both detected his hand at work a lot more often than many people did.

For Anna's mom, he was her light in the darkest times. For Anna, he was the loving Father she could always count on. His ways might be mysterious, but neither of them ever doubted that God always knew exactly what he was doing.

Of course, being homeless had been a pretty big pill for Anna to swallow. There was so much about it *not* to like. On the other hand, she'd also met some wonderful people, and learned a lot about courage and determination and kindness. *Maybe that's the reason I'm here. Besides, there's no law that says we have to stay homeless!*

In fact, Anna and her mom were both working very hard to change things. Mary Crawford's asthma was a lot better since she'd started treatment at the Free Clinic, and she was enrolled in a job training program. "Once I have some skills, I'll be able to get a decent job and save up for a place of our own," she said.

For Anna, it was school. She was determined to learn all she could, as fast as she could. And she wasn't stopping with just a high-school diploma, either; Anna was going to college some day! She had no idea *how* that would happen. But she was doing her part to make sure it *could* happen.

So, yes, she'd work as hard on this social studies project as she did in all her classes, *and* she'd get a top grade—without, of course, giving away her own secret advantage. After all, when it comes to understanding homelessness, there's absolutely no substitute for personal experience!

❋ ❋ ❋ In the wilderness, Christ continued his role as your stand-in, your substitute. He did for you what my friend Bobby Aycock did for David in boot camp back in 1959. David was a very likable, yet physically disadvantaged, soldier. He had the desire but not the strength. There was simply no way he would pass the fitness test. Too weak for the pull-ups.

But Bobby had such a fondness for David that he came up with a plan. He donned his friend's T-shirt. The shirt bore David's last name, two initials, and service serial number. The superiors didn't know faces; they just read the names and numbers off the shirts and marked scores on a list of names. So Bobby did David's pull-ups. David came out looking pretty good and never even broke a sweat.

> **God gives you Jesus' wilderness grade.**

Neither did you. Listen, you and I are no match for Satan. Jesus knows this. So he donned our jersey. Better still, he put on our flesh. He was "tempted in every way, just as we are—yet was without sin" (Hebrews 4:15 NIV). And because he did, we pass with flying colors.

God gives you Jesus' wilderness grade. Believe that. Trust his work.

And trust his Word. Don't trust your emotions. Don't trust your opinions. Don't even trust your friends. In the wilderness, heed only the voice of God.

Again, Jesus is our model. Remember how Satan teased him? "If you are the Son of God . . ." (Luke 4:3, 9 NCV). Why would Satan say this? Because he knew what Christ had heard at the baptism. "This is My beloved Son, in whom I am well-pleased" (Matthew 3:17).

- "Are you really God's Son?" Satan is asking. Then comes the dare—"Prove it!" Prove it by doing something:

- "Tell this stone to become bread" (Luke 4:3).

- "If You worship before me, it shall all be Yours" (Luke 4:7).

- "Throw Yourself down from here" (Luke 4:9).

What a sneak! Satan doesn't denounce God; he simply raises doubts about God. Is his work enough? Earthly works—like bread changing or temple jumping—are given equal billing with heavenly works. Satan attempts to shift our source of confidence away from God's promise and toward *our* performance.

Jesus doesn't bite the bait. No heavenly sign is requested. He doesn't solicit a lightning bolt; he simply quotes the Bible. Three temptations. Three declarations.

- "It is written . . ." (Luke 4:4 NCV).

- "It is written . . ." (Luke 4:8 NCV).

- "It is said . . ." (Luke 4:12).

Jesus' survival weapon of choice is Scripture. If the Bible was enough for his wilderness, shouldn't it be enough for ours? Don't miss the point here. Everything you and I need for desert survival is in the Book. We simply need to heed it.

"You choose tonight, Anna," said her mom, handing her the tattered Bible that had become their "field guide" to life.

"Maybe something about being thankful?" Anna suggested as she leafed through the familiar pages. "There's a lot of that going around these days," she added with a smile. Indeed, there was.

Anna's mom had finished her job training course, and she was scheduled to have her first interview tomorrow. And the class project on homelessness that Anna had such qualms about last fall had provided as many surprises for Anna as for her classmates.

True, all the kids *had* been really uncomfortable during their first shelter visits. But who'd have dreamed that instead of looking down on the people they met, they'd actually start identifying with them?! *Or* be so fierce in their determination to "do something about it!"?

Their warm-hearted response was so genuine that Anna had found it harder and harder to keep her secret—or her distance. Even worse, she was no longer sure she wanted to—it *would* be nice to have some real friends. Still . . .

Still . . . what, Anna? Still afraid they'll see a "problem" instead of a person? Still rather hide than take a chance? That last question was a real eye-opener for Anna. So was the Scripture her absent-minded fingers had settled on. John 8:32 practically leaped off the page! "The truth will make you free." *Oh, my.*

❊ ❊ ❊

The session in which they recorded their CD about the homeless was one that no one in Miss Marsh's social studies class would ever forget. One by one, they each took a turn at the microphone—to become the "voice" of someone they'd met or heard about at the shelters. Then it was Anna's turn.

"My name is Anna," she began in a slightly unsteady voice. "I'm fourteen years old. And I don't have to *imagine* what it's like to be homeless. I know. Because I am." Then she took a deep breath and lifted her chin.

"But . . . ," she continued, her voice ringing like a bell, "that's not *all* I am. My father is the King of heaven, and the way I see it, that makes *me* a princess! Of course"—and here a smile tugged at the corners of her mouth—"we princesses *do* have our responsibilities. Mine is to make the best of what I have; make the most of every day; and make *me* the best Anna I can possibly be.

"That's not to say," she added, grinning outright, "that my current 'castle' couldn't use a little work."

For a long moment there was silence. Then the applause began.

❊ ❊ ❊ On a trip to the United Kingdom, our family visited a castle. In the center of the garden sat a maze. Row after row of shoulder-high hedges, leading to one dead end after another. Successfully navigate the labyrinth, and discover the door to a tall tower in the center of the garden. Were you to look at our family pictures of the trip, you'd see four of our five family members standing on the top of the tower. Hmm, someone is still on the ground. Guess who? I was stuck in the foliage. I just couldn't figure out which way to go.

Ah, but then I heard a voice from above.

Ah, but then I heard a voice from above. "Hey, Dad." I looked up to see Sara, peering through the turret at the top. "You're going the wrong way," she explained. "Back up and turn right."

Do you think I trusted her? I didn't have to. I could have trusted my own instincts, consulted other confused tourists, sat and pouted and wondered why God would let this happen to me. But do you know what I did? I listened. Her vantage point was better than mine. She was above the maze. She could see what I couldn't.

Don't you think we should do the same with God? "God is . . . higher than the heavens" (Job 22:12 TLB). "The Lord is high above all nations" (Psalm 113:4). Can he not see what eludes us? Doesn't he want to get us out and bring us home? Then we should do what Jesus did.

Rely on Scripture. Doubt your doubts before you doubt your beliefs. Jesus told Satan, "Man shall not live on bread alone, but on every word that proceeds out of the mouth of God" (Matthew 4:4). The verb *proceeds* literally means "pouring out." Its tense suggests that God is constantly and aggressively communicating with the world through his Word. God is speaking still!

Hang in there. Your time in the desert will pass. Jesus' did. "The devil left Him; and behold, angels came and began to minister to Him" (Matthew 4:11).

Till angels come to you:

- *Trust his Word.* Just like me in the maze, you need a voice to lead you out.

- *Trust his work.* Like David at boot camp, you need a friend to take your place.

- Thank God you have One who will.

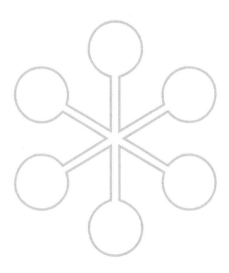

Peter said to Him, "Lord, if it is You, command me to come to You on the water."

And He said, "Come!" And Peter got out of the boat, and walked on the water and came toward Jesus. But seeing the wind, he became frightened, and beginning to sink, he cried out, "Lord, save me!"

Immediately Jesus stretched out His hand and took hold of him, and said to him, "You of little faith, why did you doubt?"

—Matthew 14:28–31

❋ ❋ ❋ On a September morning in 2001, Frank Silecchia laced up his boots, pulled on his hat, and headed out the door of his New Jersey house. As a construction worker, he made a living making things. But as a volunteer at the World Trade

Center wreckage site, he just tried to make sense of it all. He hoped to find a live body. He did not. He found forty-seven dead ones.

Amid the destruction, however, he stumbled upon a symbol—a twenty-foot-tall steel-beam cross. The collapse of Tower One onto Building Six created a crude chamber in the clutter. In the chamber, through the dusty sunrise, Frank spotted the cross.

No winch had hoisted it; no cement secured it. The iron beams stood independent of human help. Standing alone, but not alone. Other crosses rested randomly at the base of the large one. Different sizes, different angles, but all crosses.

"Where is God in all this?"

Several days later, engineers realized the beams of the large cross came from two different buildings. When one crashed into another, the two girders bonded into one, forged by the fire.[5]

A symbol in the shards. A cross found in the crisis. "Where is God in all this?" we asked. The discovery dared us to hope, "Right in the middle of it all."

"But how can they hate us so much? They don't even know us!" That was Erin, who tended to take *everything* very personally. Even so, her question was a good one—and the start of something very special.

Like kids everywhere, the Highland Church youth group

was still struggling to make some kind of sense of September 11, 2001. Never mind that many months lay between then and now; that terrible day was indelibly engraved on every mind. Being the object of hatred has that effect. So does the feeling that you're at the mercy of things you can't control.

What *could* a bunch of teens do about any of those things?!

Terrorism. War. The deep differences that set one people against another. What *could* a bunch of teens do about any of those things?! Not much it seemed, except maybe keep their heads down and hope it wouldn't happen again. Which was hardly a comforting strategy.

It was Marc who got things going. "But what if they could?" he speculated, still thinking about Erin's question.

"What if *who* could *what*?" demanded Erin, her feathers still ruffled at the thought of being so . . . hated.

"The people you were talking about," Marc answered absently, still pursuing his thought. "What if they *could* know us, and what if we could know *them* . . . ? You know, just see each other as . . . people?"

"Let me get this straight," tossed in Jay, the self-appointed naysayer of the group. "We transport halfway around the world and—what?—say something like, 'Hi, I'm not the selfish, lazy, *rich* person you think I am. And you're not the ignorant, violent barbarian I think you are. Wanna do lunch?'"

"Kind of." Marc grinned, well used to his buddy's love of poking at an idea just to see what would happen. "Though I did think we might start a *little* closer to home. Aren't there people right here whose language, or culture, or beliefs make us . . . uncomfortable?"

"You know . . . ," said Faith, "I think Marc's on to something. Since it's differences that divide people, shouldn't we be looking for a way around or across those differences?" The buzz that followed indicated that Faith was on to something, too.

"I don't know," tossed in Jay, just to keep things interesting. "That's a pretty big . . . river . . . to cross. And last time I looked, none of *us* could walk on water!"

"No," zinged back Faith, "but we know Someone who can. And I'll bet he's an expert bridge builder, too!"

❋ ❋ ❋ Can we find God in our tragedies, too? When sorrow takes our joy or disaster takes our hope or betrayal takes our trust—can we, like Frank at the World Trade Center, find Christ in the crisis? The presence of troubles doesn't surprise us. The absence of God, however, undoes us.

We can deal with the ambulance if God is in it.
We can stomach the hospital if God is in it.
We can face the empty house if God is in it.
Is he?

Matthew would like to answer that question for you. The walls falling around him were made of water. No roof collapsed, but it seemed as though the sky had.

A storm on the Sea of Galilee was akin to a sumo wrestler's

belly flop in a kiddy pool. The northern valley acted like a wind tunnel, funneling squalls onto the lake. Waves as tall as ten feet were common.

The account begins at nightfall. Jesus is on the mountain in prayer, and the disciples are in the boat in fear. They are "far away from land . . . fighting heavy waves" (Matthew 14:24 NLT). When does Christ come to them? At three o'clock in the morning! (Matthew 14:25 NLT). If "evening" began at six o'clock, and Christ came at three in the morning, the disciples were alone in the storm for nine hours! Nine miserable hours. Long enough for more than one disciple to ask, "Where is Jesus? He knows we are in the boat. For heaven's sake, it was his idea. Is God anywhere near?"

And from within the storm comes an unmistakable voice: "I am."

Wet robe, soaked hair. Waves slapping his waist and rain stinging his face. Jesus speaks to them at once. "Take courage! I AM! Stop being afraid!" (Matthew 14:27 AMP).

The wording sounds odd, doesn't it? "I am here" or "It is I" feels more complete. But what Jesus shouted in the storm was simply: "I AM."

The words ring like a royal fanfare. We've heard them before.

Speaking from a burning bush to a knee-knocking Moses, God announced, "I AM WHO I AM" (Exodus 3:14).

Double-dog-daring his enemies to prove him otherwise, Jesus declared, "Before Abraham was born, I am" (John 8:58).

Determined to say it often enough and loud enough to get our attention, Christ chorused:

- "I am the bread of life" (John 6:48).

- "I am the Light of the world" (John 8:12).

- "I am the gate; whoever enters through me will be saved" (John 10:9 NIV).

- "I am the good shepherd" (John 10:11).

- "I am God's Son" (John 10:36 NCV).

- "I am the resurrection and the life" (John 11:25).

- "I am the way, and the truth, and the life" (John 14:6).

- "I am the true vine" (John 15:1).

Jesus . . . the *present-tense* Christ!

"There's no time like the present!" If the Highland Church youth group *had* bothered with a motto, that would have been it. Once they sank their teeth into an idea, they rarely wasted any time making it *happen*. Now that they'd stopped worrying about how to "fix" the entire world, doing something about the differences that separated people right here at home suddenly seemed very . . . possible.

The only question was "what?" How *do* you show people that differences aren't something to be afraid of, but something to appreciate, even *celebrate?*

"Well," said Erin, "we could throw a party." She loved parties.

Yes! That was it. A party. But not just any party. They'd throw the party to end all parties . . . in the town square . . . and invite everyone to come meet the "neighbors they didn't know"! The event even already had a name, thanks to Faith. "Bridges," they'd call it—adding "A Celebration of Differences," just to make things perfectly clear.

Now all they had to do was . . . *do* it. And even that all came together so neatly it was almost as if some benevolent hand was smoothing the way.

The newspaper and radio stations jumped at the chance to be sponsors. The International Club at the local college guaranteed all the music, dance, and exotic native garb they could possibly want. The school board and Council of Churches provided a long list of immigrant families—which were bound to include some *really* good cooks—to be personally invited to add *their* specialties to the mix.

> **They realized they'd have people from fifty-three countries participating!**

When the dust settled, they realized they'd have people from fifty-three countries participating!

"Wow . . . ," said Jay, "major culture shock. Which is fine," he added quickly, "but aren't things getting—"

"Speaking of culture shock," interrupted Faith, grining at the brilliantly clashing colors in Jay's shirt—one of several eye-poppers from his always-startling wardrobe.

"Hey," he said, "I thought we *liked* colorful differences. But seriously"—a first for Jay—"aren't things getting a little *too* big?"

"Funny you should mention that," said Faith. "It *is* getting too big for just us. We definitely need help. Fortunately . . ."

And before Jay knew what had happened, *he* was in charge of coordinating all the other youth groups that wanted to be involved!

"After all," said Faith, "who better to keep things on track than someone with your talent for spotting possible glitches?" And she handed him a long list of names and numbers. "Better get going," she added. "After all, there's no—"

"Yeah, I know," said Jay, who knew better than to argue with a determined Faith, "'there's no time like the present.'"

✳ ✳ ✳ Jesus operates—always—in the present tense! He never says, "I was." We do. We do because "we were." We were younger, faster, prettier. People tend to think in the past tense, looking back on what was. Not God. Unwavering in strength, he need never say, "I was." Heaven has no rearview mirrors.

Or crystal balls. Our "I am" God never yearns, "Someday I will be."

Again, we do. Dream-fueled, we reach for horizons. "Someday I will . . ." Not God. Can water be wetter? Can wind be windless? Can God be more God? No. He does not change. He is the "I am" God. "Jesus Christ is the same yesterday, today, and forever" (Hebrews 13:8 NLT).

From the center of the storm, the unchanging Jesus shouts, "I AM." Tall in the Trade Tower wreckage. Bold against the Galilean waves. In troubled times and troubled minds, tests of courage, tests of honor—whatever your storm, "I AM."

The construction of Matthew's Scripture passage about the storm on the Sea of Galilee is made of two acts, each six verses long. The first, verses 22–27, centers on the power walk of Jesus. The second, verses 28–33, centers on the faith walk of Peter.

In the first act, Christ strides across the waves and declares the words engraved on every wise heart: "Take courage! I AM! Stop being afraid!" In the second act, a desperate disciple takes a step of faith and—for a moment—does what Christ does. He walks on water. Then he takes his eyes away from Christ and does what we do. He falls.

Two acts. Each with six verses. Each set of six verses contains ninety Greek words. And right in between the two acts, the two sets of verses, and the 180 words is this two-word declaration: "I AM."

Jesus—soaked but strong. Jesus—the "I AM" God. Whether in the words or the world, Jesus—in the midst of it all.

God gets into things! Red Seas. Big fish. Lion's dens and furnaces. Hospitals and jail cells. Judean wildernesses, weddings, funerals, and Galilean tempests. Look, and you'll find what everyone from Moses to Martha discovered: God in the middle of our storms.

That includes yours.

It was a real frog-strangler of a rainstorm that blew through town the night before the Bridges festival. But it didn't dampen the spirits of the Highland Church youth group. They were positive that the One who painted creation in an infinite variety of colors wouldn't spoil *their* "Celebration of Differences."

They were right. When they showed up bright and early the next day to set up booths, stages, and banners, they were greeted by a glorious rainbow—and a freshly washed town square.

By 10:00 A.M., when the first hesitant participants began drifting in, the day outshown even Jay's most garish shirt— which he *was* wearing. Things started slowly, of course. Ethnic groups tended to cluster together, each a little cautious about making the first move. But with the organizers energetically mixing things up, the "edges" of the various groups soon blurred, then disappeared.

Next thing you knew, an Iranian carpenter was helping a Korean grandma with a wobbly table. A Hispanic mom returned a wandering toddler to his worried Swedish dad. Three beaming Sudanese teens were clapping to the beat of an Irish hand drum. Soon, abayas and saris were rubbing shoulders with kaftans and T-shirts; mothers of all colors were admiring each other's children; artisans brought out their handwork; and the tantalizing aromas of cuisine from around the world began wafting into the air.

Then the music started. By the time the townsfolk showed up for the party, the square was a kaleidoscope of color and laughter and friendly—if not always understandable—chatter in dozens of languages. Which made it kind of impossible not to just . . . jump in and join the fun. So they did. Although there were some startled looks at the realization that all this had been here all the time—right under their noses. Imagine that.

Imagine, too, what happens when you stop being suspicious of differences and start enjoying them. Imagine what happens when you realize that *you* might seem as "exotic" to someone else as he does to you. Imagine what happens when you discover the awesome power of a friendly smile to bridge all *kinds* of differences. That day, an entire town did—and was never the same again.

> **Imagine what happens when you stop being suspicious of differences and start enjoying them.**

"Isn't it great?" Jay beamed, swallowing a mouthful of sushi. "Glad I thought of it," he added with a teasing look at Erin, who obligingly sputtered. Then, snitching a piece of baklava from Faith's plate, he beat a strategic retreat. "Gotta run, haven't tried the falafel yet."

Faith just laughed as she watched the green-orange-purple glory of Jay's shirt merge into the rainbow swirl of people who were making an amazing discovery: They really weren't that different after all . . . *inside!* And somewhere—right in the middle of the joyful confusion—if you looked very carefully, Faith knew, you could see God.

�֎ �֎ ✖ During the days this book was written, a young woman died in our city. She was recently married, the mother of an eighteen-month-old. Her life seemed abbreviated. The shelves of help and hope go barren at such times. But at the funeral, the officiating priest shared a memory in his eulogy that gave both.

For several years the woman had lived and worked in New York City. Due to their long friendship, the priest stayed in constant touch with her via e-mail. Late one night he received a message demonstrating God's persistent presence.

She had missed her station on the subway. By the time she realized her mistake, she didn't know what to do. She prayed for safety and some sign of God's presence. This was no hour or place for a young, attractive woman to be passing through a rough neighborhood alone. At that moment the doors opened, and a homeless, disheveled man came on board and plopped down next to her. *God? Are you near?* she prayed. The answer came in a song. The man pulled out a harmonica and played, "Be Thou My Vision"—her mother's favorite hymn.

The song was enough to convince her. Christ was there, in the midst of it all.

The construction worker saw him in the rubble. Matthew saw him in the waves. And you? Look closer. He's there. Right in the middle of it all.

Chapter 14

Christ's Point of View [God-Blessed Places]

LUKE 21:37

During the day He was teaching in the temple, but at evening He would go out and spend the night on the mount that is called Olivet.

—Luke 21:37

✻✻✻ A man and his dog are in the same car. The dog howls rock-concert-volume complaints. The man pleads, promising a daily delivery of dog-biscuit bouquets if only the hound will hush. After all, it's only a car wash.

Never occurred to him—ahem, me—that the car wash would scare the dog. But it did. Placing myself in her paws, I can see why. A huge, noisy machine presses toward us, pounding our window with water, banging against the door with brushes. *Duck! We're under attack!*

"Don't panic. The car wash was my idea." "I've done this

before." "It's for our own good." Ever tried to explain a car wash to a canine? Dog dictionaries are minus the words *brush* and *detail job*. My words fell on fallen earflaps. Nothing helped. Molly just did what dogs do; she wailed.

> God's greatest blessings often come costumed as disasters.

Actually, she did what *we* do. Don't we howl? Not at car washes, perhaps, but at hospital stays and lost opportunities. Let our team lose or a friend disappoint us, and we have a wail of a time. And when our Master explains what's happening, we react as if he's speaking Yalunka. We don't understand a word he says.

Is your world wet and wild?

Take heart; God's greatest blessings often come costumed as disasters.

When he thought about it later, Craig felt pretty embarrassed about his *first* reaction to Tuesday morning's disaster.

Of course, at the time, he had no idea how much damage had been done by the tornado that ripped through town. His neighborhood was spared; so Craig just assumed that it was an especially nasty late-spring thunderstorm.

Besides—what with missing his mom, and thinking about the exciting weekend ahead—he had other things on his mind. Until . . . until the lights flickered, then steadied; the sirens started; and the reports began coming in from the first news crews on the scene.

Soon, like everyone else in the parts of town that still had power, Craig and his dad were glued to the TV. Nothing made much sense at first. Images of caught-off-guard weather specialists, drenched field reporters, and hastily edited footage of fallen trees, overturned cars, and roofs on lawns (!) whizzed by in a confusing blur. Finally, the National Weather Service called it by name.

A tornado? Here?! While Craig was getting used to *that* news, Channel 4 switched to a shot of a badly damaged building. *Why, that looks like . . . my school! But . . . but where's the music wing?*

Where, indeed? Most of Marshall Consolidated School looked perfectly fine—until the camera zoomed in on the neatly sliced-off north end of the building. There, instead of the music wing that was the town's pride and joy, was nothing but a huge pile of rubble. And buried somewhere beneath it all had to be the gleaming instruments and spiffy new uniforms that were supposed to have marched to victory at this weekend's State Championship Battle of the Bands!

Craig was stunned by the sight. Forget tornadoes! *This* was serious. (Okay, it *was* kind of a shallow reaction. But you had to understand where Craig—and, indeed, the whole town—was coming from when it came to their band.)

Marshall might not be all that big a town, but their kids had been a major force for decades in state, regional, and national band competitions. Over the years, the Marshall Mavericks had packed the school trophy case with more awards than they could count—and they'd made it all the way to the Grand National Championships nine times!

When the Mavericks took the field, their inspired playing and brilliant precision marching were awesome—and they worked themselves relentlessly to keep up the tradition. And *nobody* had worked harder than Craig in getting ready for this weekend's state championships.

As the youngest-ever field commander in Mavericks history, Craig felt a special responsibility to make this year their best showing ever. Finally—after months of we'll-do-it-till-we-get-it-right! practice—the Mavericks had the most dazzling, quick-stepping extravaganza of marching band perfection that anyone could remember. It was bound to be the talk of the state championships. Or *would* have been—except for an ill-timed tornado!

We worked so hard! What was God thinking?! Craig fumed. He was so focused on his band's "disaster" that he was barely aware of the one unfolding on TV. But then there were a *lot* of things about disasters Craig wasn't aware of . . . yet.

❋ ❋ ❋ Let me repeat: God's greatest blessings often come costumed as disasters. Any doubters need to do nothing more than ascend the hill of Calvary.

Jerusalem's collective opinion that Friday was this: Jesus was finished. What other conclusion made sense? The religious leaders had turned him in. Rome had refused to bail him out. His followers had tucked their tails and scattered. He was nailed to a cross and left to die, which he did. They silenced his lips, sealed his tomb, and, as any priest who knew his way around the temple would tell you, Jesus was history. Three years of power and promises were silent in a borrowed grave. Search the crucifixion sky for one ray of hope, and you wouldn't find it. Such was the view of the disciples, the opinion of the friends, and the outlook of the enemies. Label it the dog-in-the-passenger-seat view.

The Master who sits behind the wheel thought differently.

The Master who sits behind the wheel thought differently. God was not surprised. His plan was right on schedule. Even in—*especially* in—death, Christ was still the King, the King over his own crucifixion.

Want proof?

During his final twenty-four hours on earth, what one word did Jesus speak the most? Search these verses for a repeated phrase:

- "I, the Son of Man, must die, as the Scriptures declared long ago" (Matthew 26:24 NLT).

- "Tonight all of you will desert me," Jesus told them. "For the Scriptures say, 'God will strike the Shepherd, and the sheep of the flock will be scattered'" (Matthew 26:31 NLT).

- He could have called thousands of angels to help him but didn't, for this reason: "If I did, how would the Scriptures be fulfilled that describe what must happen now?" (Matthew 26:54 NLT).

- Rather than blame the soldiers who arrested him, he explained that they were players in a drama they didn't write. "But this is all happening to fulfill the words of the prophets as recorded in the Scriptures" (Matthew 26:56 NLT).

- "The Scriptures declare, 'The one who shares my food has turned against me,' and this will soon come true" (John 13:18 NLT).

- To his heavenly Father he prayed: "I guarded them so that not one was lost, except the one headed for destruction, as the Scriptures foretold" (John 17:12 NLT).

- He said to them, "The Scripture says, 'He was treated like a criminal,' and I tell you this scripture must have its full meaning. It was written about me, and it is happening now" (Luke 22:37 NCV).

Do you detect it? *Scripture. Love, sacrifice,* and *devotion* are terms we might expect. But *Scripture* leads the list and reveals this truth: Jesus arranged his final days to fulfill Old Testament prophecies. As if he was following a mental list, Jesus checked them off one by one.

Why did Scripture matter to Christ? And why does it matter to us that it mattered to him? Because he loves the Thomases among us. While others kneel and worship, you stroke your chin and wonder if you could see some proof. "How can I know the death of Christ is anything more than the death of a man?"

Begin with the fulfilled prophecy. More Old Testament fore-tellings were fulfilled during the Crucifixion than on any other day. Twenty-nine different prophecies, the youngest of which was five hundred years old, were completed on the day of Christ's death. Want some examples?

- But he was wounded for the wrong things we did. He was crushed for the evil things we did. The punish-ment, which made us well, was given to him. And we are healed because of his wounds. (Isaiah 53:5 ICB)

- They pierced My hands and My feet. (Psalm 22:16 NKJV)

- "And it shall come to pass in that day," says the LORD GOD, "that I will make the sun go down at noon, and I will darken the earth in broad daylight" (Amos 8:9 NKJV).[6]

Daylight never seemed to fully arrive that Tuesday. Long after the tornado had passed, a constant downpour—and power out-ages in many areas of town—maintained a dreary twilight gloom. The steadily growing reports of damage weren't exactly mood-brighteners, either. But they did, finally, help Craig see things in a different light.

As the extent of the disaster unfolded on TV, a missed trip to a band competition started to seem like pretty small pota-toes. A lot of people had lost so much more! While he sat in a house with heat and light—and a refrigerator that worked—many were wondering how they'd manage without roofs and walls, or dinner.

No lives had been lost, but the cleanup job ahead was . . . mind-boggling. The thing was, how *do* you clean up a mess like this? But then, bringing order out of chaos—getting a hundred and fifty pair of enthusiastic feet to march in perfect step—was Craig's specialty. And it wasn't long before he was itching to "get out there and *do something!*"

"Patience," said his dad. "The smart thing today is to stay put while the emergency crews do their work."

Craig couldn't argue with that, but . . . , "It sure is hard just watching from the sidelines."

"Don't worry, " came Dad's reply while they watched shots of the destruction on Elm Street, "tomorrow there'll be plenty for everybody to do. Besides, there's nothing to keep your *brain* from getting to work right now."

Dad's right: before the muscle work, the groundwork! If only . . . Yes! . . . the phone still worked. By bedtime, Craig had reached every band member who was reachable. They all jumped at the chance, and agreed to meet at eight in the morning . . . outside their school's used-to-be music wing. From there, they'd head out to wherever the Volunteer Hotline sent them.

Craig's walk over to school Wednesday morning was an adventure in itself. There were trees—*enormous* trees—down everywhere.

On roofs. On unlucky cars. On yards and streets. And where there weren't trees, there were huge limbs, piles of shingles, and gobs of soaked insulation everywhere you looked. Such a mess. Such a challenge. Such an *opportunity*—to give something back to the town that had given them so much.

With Craig calling the tune, the Marshall Mavericks swung into action—and performed like champions wherever the work was hardest and dirtiest.

> *Strange,* he thought. *What tore things apart also brought people together!*

Of course, they weren't the only ones. People came from all over town to help those who hadn't been as lucky as they were. And in the hard-hit areas, neighbors who'd only nodded before now traded damage reports, gave each other a hand, and decided that "Hey, it could be worse." All of which Craig found as impressive as the amount of damage.

Strange, he thought, dragging a limb from the street. *What tore things apart also brought people together!* That was the *first* thing he learned about disasters. Not that there was a lot of time for philosophical reflection—*or* missing your mom, *or* worrying about minor details like state championships.

The next days passed in a blur of hard work, aching muscles, and shared accomplishment—all set to the weird background music of buzzing chain saws. In fact, Craig wouldn't even have noticed that the weekend—the state championship weekend!—had arrived at all, if it hadn't been for the surprising change of circumstances at home.

❊ ❊ ❊ As terrible as the Crucifixion was, don't call Jesus a victim of circumstances. Call him a controller of circumstances! He guided the actions of his enemies to fulfill prophecy. And he used the tongues of his enemies to declare truth.

Christ rarely spoke on that Friday. He didn't need to. His accusers provided accurate play-by-play. Remember the sign nailed to the cross?

> Pilate posted a sign over him that read, "Jesus of Nazareth, the King of the Jews." The place where Jesus was crucified was near the city; and the sign was written in Hebrew, Latin, and Greek, so that many people could read it. (John 19:19–20 NLT)

Truth in three languages. Thank you, Pilate, for funding the first advertising campaign of the Cross and introducing Jesus as the King of the Jews.

And thanks to the Pharisees for the sermon:

> He saved others; himself he cannot save.
> (Matthew 27:42 KJV)

Could the words be more on-target? Jesus could not, at the same time, save others and save himself. So he saved others.

The award for the most unlikely spokesman goes to the high priest. Caiaphas said, "It is better for one man to die for the people than for the whole nation to be destroyed" (John 11:50 NCV).

Was Caiaphas a believer? Sure sounds like one. Indeed, it *was* better for Christ to die than for all of us to perish. Heaven gets no argument from him. You'd almost think heaven caused him to say what he said. If that's what you think, you are right.

> Caiaphas did not think of this himself. As high priest that year, he was really prophesying that Jesus would die for the Jewish nation and for God's scattered children to bring them all together and make them one. (John 11:51–52 NCV)

What's going on here? Caiaphas preaching for Christ? The Pharisees explaining the Cross? Pilate painting evangelistic billboards? Out of tragedy emerges triumph. Every disaster proves to be a victory.

This turn of events reminds me of the mule in the well. A mule tumbled down a water shaft. The villagers compared the effort of a rescue with the value of the animal and decided to bury him. They started shoveling dirt. The mule had other ideas. As the clods hit his back, he shook them off and stomped them down. Each spade of earth lifted him higher. He reached the top of the well and walked out. What his would-be killers thought would bury him actually delivered him.

The men who murdered Jesus did the same. Their actions elevated Jesus. Everything—the bad and the good, the evil and the decent—worked together just as Christ had planned.

Everything worked together Friday evening to catch Craig completely by surprise.

As he walked slowly up his front steps—hey, after days of manual labor, "slowly" was the best he could do—all he could think of was a long, hot shower. And dinner, naturally. Some of his mom's Secret Recipe Chili would be perfect right about now. In fact, just thinking about it, he could practically *smell* it.

Don't I wish! he thought with a tired grin as he opened the front door and walked right into—*Mom?!* Craig blinked. Then blinked again. No, he wasn't hallucinating. There, in the front hall, stood his mom—his mom who was supposed to be at National Guard Camp three states away!

"Hello, sweetheart," she said with a smile, "dinner's rea—"

The rest of her words were lost somewhere inside Craig's bear hug. "But . . . but what are you doing *here?*"

"Well," she said when she could breathe again, "that's kind of an interesting story. I'll tell you over dinner."

Not only was it an interesting story—six months' worth of catching up—but it was also a good news/bad news story. The good news: She had three whole days at home on a surprise leave! The bad news: The visit home was because her National Guard Unit was shipping out to the Middle East the next week!

Now, that last bit of news *could* fall into the "disaster" category. But Craig had learned a thing or two about disasters this week—and the surprising silver linings inside even the darkest clouds.

Why, if there hadn't *been a tornado . . . and I* had *been out of town all weekend at the band competition . . . I'd have missed this time with Mom!* So who could say, for sure, what was—or wasn't—a disaster?

After all, God *does* have quite a way with surprises.

✻ ✻ ✻ Should we be surprised at the way everything in the Crucifixion worked out as Christ had planned? Didn't he promise this would happen? "We know that in everything God works for the good of those who love him" (Romans 8:28 NCV).

Everything? Everything. Chicken-hearted disciples. A two-timing Judas. A pierced side. Spineless Pharisees. A hard-hearted high priest. In everything God worked. I dare you to find one element of the Cross that he did not manage for good or recycle for symbolism. Give it a go. I think you'll find what I found—every dark detail was actually a golden moment in the cause of Christ.

Can't he do the same for you? Can't he turn your sad Friday into a joyful Sunday?

Can you imagine the difference between the wisdom of a human and the wisdom of God?

Some of you doubt it. How can God use cancer or death or divorce? Simple.

He's smarter than we are. He is to you what I was to four-year-old Amy. I met her at a bookstore. She asked me if I would sign her children's book. When I asked her name, she watched as I began to write, "To Amy . . ."

She stopped me right there. With wide eyes and open mouth, she asked, "How did you know how to spell my name?"

She was awed. You aren't. You know the difference between the knowledge of a child and an adult. Can you imagine the difference between the wisdom of a human and the wisdom of God? What is impossible to us is like spelling "Amy" to him. "For as the heavens are higher than the earth, so are My ways higher than your ways and My thoughts than your thoughts" (Isaiah 55:9).

I keep taking my dog Molly to the car wash. She's howling less. I don't think she understands the machinery. She's just learning to trust her master.

Maybe we'll learn the same.

CHAPTER 15

STILL IN THE NEIGHBORHOOD (NEAR ENOUGH TO TOUCH, STRONG ENOUGH TO TRUST.)

MATTHEW 28:20 NIV

Surely I am with you always, to the very end of the age.
—Matthew 28:20 NIV

❋ ❋ ❋ Soon after September 11, 2001, a group of religious leaders were invited by the White House to come to Washington and pray with the president. How my name got on the list, who knows. But I was happy to accept. Thirty or so of us were seated in a room.

The group was well frocked and well known. Several Catholic cardinals. The president of the Mormon Church and a leader of the Bahai faith. Esteemed Jewish and Muslim spokesmen. An impressive cross section of religious leadership.

You might wonder if I felt out of place. I lead no denomination. The only time I wear a robe is when I step out of the shower. No one calls me "The Right Most Reverend Lucado."

(Although my wife, Denalyn, promises me she will. Once. Someday. Before I die.)

Did I feel like a minnow in a whale's world? Hardly. I was special among them. And when my turn came to meet George W. Bush, I had to mention why. After giving my name, I added, "And, Mr. President, I was raised in Andrews, Texas." For those of you whose subscription to *National Geographic* has expired, Andrews is only a half-hour drive from Midland, the president's hometown. Upon learning that we were neighbors, he hitched his britches and smiled that lopsided smile and let his accent drawl ever so slightly. "Why, I know your town. I've walked those streets. I've even played your golf course."

I stood a tad taller. It's nice to know that the most powerful man in the world has walked my streets.

How much nicer to know the same about God.

Yes, he is in heaven. Yes, he rules the universe. But, yes, he has walked your streets. He's still the next door Savior. Near enough to touch. Strong enough to trust.

She'd just have to trust in God . . . and her gift; that was all there was to it! *After all, what else do I really need?* But, oh, my, she wished this ordeal was over!

Leslie Morrison had a bad case of audition nerves. Sweaty hands, unsettled stomach, shaky knees; she didn't miss a symptom as she waited her turn—forever, it seemed—outside the recital hall. She was usually a confident performer who loved sharing her gift, but then, this was no ordinary audition.

Her entire future—or so she believed—hinged on today's result.

Music had been the passion and focus of Leslie's life for most of her fourteen years. She was well aware that her extraordinary talent was a gift from God and deserved the best she had to give. She gave it gladly, throwing herself into pursuing her dream of becoming a concert violinist. Winning one of the coveted places in the Arts High School would be a major step toward that goal.

AHS was nationally known for its excellent advanced training, outstanding academics, and demanding admission requirements. There were only a few openings in the music program each year, and Leslie desperately wanted one of them. Her parents had stretched themselves to the limit, but the cost of lessons and quality instruments would only grow as time passed. A place at the Arts High School would make all the difference.

But first, she had to get past the AHS Admissions Committee—and she'd heard *all* about them!

Even allowing for exaggeration, their reputation for tough standards and a pressure-makes-diamonds philosophy couldn't have happened by accident. Not that they weren't entitled. In addition to teaching at AHS, every member of the Admissions Committee was *also* a professional musician—mainstays of local and regional orchestras and concert ensembles. They respected talent. They understood commitment. They wanted excellence.

But so do I! Leslie reminded herself, pacing the cracked marble floor. *So what's the problem?* And she made herself sit down, take a deep breath, and . . . relax. After all, she'd worked for months to get ready for today. She had her audition piece down cold. And she vaguely remembered actually *enjoying* performing.

But what if . . . And Leslie was off again on another circuit of the room, pursued by random possibilities of disaster.

> **Gifted artist. Nervous schoolgirl.**

Gifted artist. Nervous schoolgirl. Two sides of the "coin" that was Leslie. And, today especially, there was no way to have one without the other!

�֍ �֍ �֍ Jesus—God *and* man. Still find the idea hard to grasp? Maybe this will help. Paul merges these two truths about Jesus, our next door Savior, into *one* promise: "Christ Jesus is He who died, yes, rather who was raised, who is at the right hand of God, who also intercedes for us" (Romans 8:34).

See his divinity? He is "at the right hand of God."

"Right hand of God" equals the highest honor. Is Jesus above all powers? You bet he is:

> He is *far above* any ruler or authority or power or leader or anything else in this world or in the world to come. And God has put all things under the authority of Christ, and he gave him this authority for the benefit of the church.
>
> And the church is his body; it is filled by Christ, who fills everything everywhere with his presence. (Ephesians 1:21–23 NLT, emphasis mine)

Christ is running the show. Right now. A leaf just fell from a tree in the Alps. Christ caused it to do so. A newborn baby in India inhaled for the first time. Jesus measured the breath. The migration of the whales through the oceans? Christ dictates their route. He is

the firstborn of all creation. For by Him all things were created, both in the heavens and on earth, visible and invisible, whether thrones or dominions or rulers or authorities—all things have been created through Him and for Him. (Colossians 1:15–16)

What a phenomenal list! Heavens and earth. Visible and invisible. Thrones, dominions, rulers, and authorities. No thing, place, or person left out. The scale on the sea urchin. The hair on the elephant hide. The hurricane that wrecks the coast, the rain that nourishes the desert, the infant's first heartbeat, the elderly person's final breath—all can be traced back to the hand of Christ, the firstborn of creation.

> ## Christ is running the show. Right now.

Firstborn in Paul's language has nothing to do with birth order. *Firstborn* refers to order of rank. As one translation states: "He ranks higher than everything that has been made" (Colossians 1:15 NCV). Everything? Find an exception. Peter's mother-in-law has a fever; Jesus dismisses it. When five thousand stomachs growl, Jesus renders a boy's lunch basket a bottomless buffet. Jesus radiates authority. He bats an eyelash, and nature jumps. No one argues when, at the end of his earthly life, the God-man declares, "All authority has been given to Me in heaven and on earth" (Matthew 28:18).

No doubt about it: Jesus is in charge.

There was no doubt about it, total strangers were in charge of her future! It was the one thought Leslie couldn't escape, no matter how many times she mentally rehearsed the violin concerto that was her audition piece. The long wait for her turn wasn't helping her jangled nerves, either. *On the other hand, maybe* not *knowing is better than . . . No! Don't even think it.* With a determined shake of her head, Leslie pushed away any thought of failure.

True, the soaring spaces of the elegant historic building that housed Arts High School *did* make her feel kind of . . . small. And, yes, the thought of all the talent that had passed through here on the way to brilliant careers was pretty intimidat-

Leslie pushed away any thought of failure.

ing. *But . . . ,* Leslie reminded herself, *they did* start *here. With an audition they probably dreaded. Just like me.*

Oddly enough, the thought of all that company for her misery did help. So did the company she had here in the Ready Room—waiting their turn to try out for the chance of a lifetime. Flutes, violins, cellos, oboes were nestled in nervous arms or sat primly by shuffling feet. Only thick piano scores filled some hands—the piano not being a very *portable* instrument. And, of course, the voice students had been born "instruments included."

Most amazing—even amusing, if you happened to be in the mood—was the way a room filled with teens could be so . . . quiet. Everyone, Leslie included, was wrapped in a cloak of nervous silence, wondering: *How will I measure up?*

Leslie tried to look on the bright side. She knew she was good—not just because others said so, but with a certainty deep inside that God had blessed her in a special way. She knew she was prepared—hours and months and *years* of practice. She knew—maybe the most important of all—that she'd been generous in using her talent to help others, too.

At the thought of the disadvantaged kids she worked with at Project Music, Leslie couldn't help but smile. Of course, "work" was hardly the word to describe the excitement of helping someone discover the *joy* of making music. Spending so many Saturdays at the Community Center's unofficial "music school" could hardly be considered a sacrifice. It was too much fun!

She'd met some wonderful people there, too—including Miss Cantrell, the volunteer director of Project Music. The tall, quiet woman with the stern face hadn't seemed that impressive at first. But once Leslie saw the way her face lit up when some struggling student "got it"—or heard her talk about the way music *glorified* life—she knew she'd met a kindred spirit.

Not that Miss Cantrell was an easy touch. She insisted that the kids treat their borrowed instruments with loving care and show up for their lessons *prepared!* "Music is too special a gift for anything but your best," she'd tell them. And the lessons weren't free, either—another Miss Cantrell idea. They cost a whole dime. "Because what you pay for, you value." Of course, Miss Cantrell was also the one who provided little chores to earn a dime. She was tough. She was demanding. And the kids all adored her. So, for that matter, did Les—

"Leslie Cantrell?" Leslie jumped. She hadn't even heard the door to the Ready Room open!

Oh, my. So soon? "Here."

Leslie breathed a silent prayer and went to meet her fate. The power to decide what happened next was out of her hands.

❊ ❊ ❊ There is no limit to God's power.

> Out of the south comes the storm. . . .
> [God] disperses the cloud of His lightning.
> It changes direction, turning around by His guidance,
> That it may do whatever He commands it
> On the face of the inhabited earth.
> Whether for correction . . .
> Or for lovingkindness, He causes it to happen. . . .
> Stand and consider the wonders of God. (Job 37:9–14)

Stand and consider, indeed.

- The Hubble Space Telescope sends back infrared images of faint galaxies that are perhaps twelve billion light-years away (twelve billion times six trillion miles).[7]

- Astronomers venture a feeble estimate that the number of stars in the universe equals the number of grains of sand on all the beaches of the world.[8]

- The star Betelgeuse has a diameter of one hundred million miles, which is larger than the earth's orbit around the sun.[9]

Why the immensity? Why such vast, unmeasured, unexplored, "unused" space? So that you and I—with the power of Jesus on our side—can be inspired by this belief: "I can do all things through Christ who strengthens me" (Philippians 4:13 NKJV).

The Christ of the galaxies is the Christ of your Mondays. The Starmaker manages your travel schedule. Relax. You have a friend in high places. Does the child of Arnold Schwarzenegger worry about tight pickle-jar lids? Does the son of Nike founder Phil Knight sweat a broken shoestring? If the daughter of Microsoft's Bill Gates can't turn on her computer, does she panic?

> **Even in heaven, Christ remains our next door Savior.**

No. Nor should you. The universe's Commander in Chief knows your name. He has walked your streets.

Even in heaven, Christ remains our next door Savior. Even in heaven, he is still "Christ Jesus . . . who died." The King of the universe commands comets with a human tongue and directs celestial traffic with a human hand.

Still human. Still divine. Living forever through his two natures.

Wait a second, Max. Are you saying that Jesus is still in his fleshly body? That angels worship what Galileans touched? Yes, indeed. Jesus appeared to the followers after his resurrection in a flesh-and-bone body: "A spirit does not have flesh and bones as you see that I have" (Luke 24:39). His resurrected body was a real body, real enough to walk on the road to Emmaus, to be mistaken for that of a gardener, to swallow fish at breakfast.

In the same breath, Jesus' real body was *really* different. The disciples didn't recognize him, and walls didn't stop him. Mark tried to describe the new look and settled for "[Jesus] appeared in another form" (Mark 16:12 NKJV). While his body was the same, it was better; it was glorified. It was a heavenly body.

And I can't find the passage that says he shed it. He ascended to heaven in it. "He was lifted up while they were looking on, and a cloud received Him out of their sight" (Acts 1:9). He will return in it. The angel told the followers, "This Jesus, who has been taken up from you into heaven, will come in just the same way as you have watched Him go into heaven" (Acts 1:11).

The God-man is still both. The hands that blessed the bread of the boy to feed the five thousand now bless the prayers of millions. And the mouth that directs angels is the mouth that kissed children.

You know what this means? The greatest force in the cosmos understands and intercedes for you. "We have an Advocate with the Father, Jesus Christ the righteous" (1 John 2:1). We have someone who speaks *for* us, directly to God!

My talent will have to speak for me today! With that thought, Leslie lifted her chin, walked out onto the stage, and faced her judges.

There they were—the dread Admissions Committee—lined up like birds on a branch in the front row of seats. Seven shadowy figures who had the power to give—or withhold—the place she yearned for in Arts High School. Seven strangers who held her future in their indifferent hands. Seven AHS teachers *and* working professionals who—

Enough with the counting, Leslie, make eye contact!

She tried her best, but the first six faces passed in kind of a blur. Then Leslie's eyes reached the seventh face. Which looked kind of—no, *very*—familiar!

Miss Cantrell?! But that couldn't be. Everyone on the Admissions Committee was some kind of big deal on the professional music scene. The only Cantrell she'd ever heard of like that was *Jemimah* Cantrell—the symphony's newly appointed first violin that everyone was so excited about! *Leslie's* Miss Cantrell was just . . . just a music teacher who probably gave lessons in her living room. Wasn't she? Or was that what Leslie had just *assumed?*

Miss Cantrell never talked much about herself. *So she could be from . . . Mars . . . for all I really know! Or . . . on the elite AHS faculty and Admissions Committee!* Leslie wasn't sure which possibility was the most unsettling. Then Miss Cantrell decided for her, with a quick smile and a . . . wink. And that made all the difference. The comfort of seeing a friendly face in a crowd of strangers settled everything—including Leslie's nerves—back into place. Not that she'd get any kind of a free pass. In fact, Miss Cantrell would probably be the toughest of all to impress.

But, of course, it's not about impressing; it's about making music. And there was all the difference in the world between performing for indifferent strangers and *sharing* her gift with people whose passion for music matched her own.

Sure and steady now, Leslie tucked her violin under her chin, lifted her bow, and smiled.

We all speak a language that needs no translation.

With a sweep of her bow, Leslie let the music speak for her. She was among friends.

❊ ❊ ❊ Sir John Clarke dedicated many years to Bible translation in the Belgian Congo. He had difficulty translating the word *advocate*. For two years he searched for a suitable translation. His search ended the day he visited the king of the Mulongo people. During the time with the king, an aide appeared, received his instructions, and left. The king told Clarke that the aide was his Nsenga Mukwashi, which was not a name, but a title.

The king explained that the servant represented the people to the king. Clarke immediately asked for permission to watch the man at work. He went to the edge of the village where he found him talking with three women. The husband of one of the women had died, and she was being evicted from her hut. She needed help.

"I will take you to the king," the Nsenga Mukwashi told her.

"Do not do that," she objected. "I am old and timid and would become speechless in his presence."

"There will be no need for you to speak," he assured her. "I shall speak for you."

And he did. Clearly and passionately. Clarke noted the flash of anger in the king's eyes. The sovereign ordered his court to care for the widow and seize the culprits who had tried to take away her home. The widow found justice, and Clarke found his word—*Nsenga Mukwashi*.[10]

You, too, have an advocate with the Father. When you are weak, he is strong. When you are timid, he speaks. Your next door Savior is your Nsenga Mukwashi.

Jesus understands every weakness of ours, because he was tempted in every way that we are. But he did not sin! So whenever we are in need, we should come bravely before the throne of our merciful God. There we will be treated with undeserved kindness, and we will find help. (Hebrews 4:15–16 CEV)

Alas, my example of meeting with President Bush falls short. Can I call him? Even if I had the number, he's too busy. Yet can I call God? Anytime. He is not too busy for me—or you. Endowed with sleepless attention and endless devotion, he listens. The fact that we can't imagine how he hears a million requests as if they were only one doesn't mean he can't or doesn't. For he can and he does.

And among the requests he hears and heeds is yours. For even though he is in heaven, he never left the neighborhood.

notes

chapter 6
1. Joni Eareckson Tada et al., *When Morning Gilds the Skies: Hymns of Heaven and Our Eternal Hope* (Wheaton, Ill.: Crossway Books, 2002), 23–24. Used by permission.

part 2
2. Paul Aurandt, *Destiny and 102 Other Real-Life Mysteries* (New York: Bantam Books, 1983), 225.

chapter 8
3. Maxie Dunnam, *This Is Christianity* (Nashville: Abingdon Press, 1994), 60–61.

chapter 10
4. Taken from Don Stephens, "Of Mercy—and Peanut Butter," The Mercy Minute, at www.mercyships.org (2003), and Harold S. McNabb Jr., "Inspirational Thoughts from the Legacy of George Washington Carver," speech at Iowa State University.

chapter 13
5. Ann Coulter, "Dressing for Distress," October 24, 2001, www.worldnetdaily.com.

chapter 14
6. Josh McDowell, *The New Evidence That Demands a Verdict* (Nashville: Thomas Nelson, 1999), 186, 189, 192.

chapter 15
7. John Piper, *Seeing and Savoring Jesus Christ* (Wheaton, Ill.: Crossway Books, 2001), 19.
8. John MacArthur Jr., *The MacArthur New Testament Commentary: Colossians and Philemon* (Chicago: Moody Press, 1992), 48.
9. MacArthur, *MacArthur New Testament Commentary: Colossians and Philemon,* 47.
10. Charles J. Rolls, *Time's Noblest Name: The Names and Titles of Jesus Christ* (Neptune, N.J.: Loizeaux Brothers, 1985), 84–86.